"IT'S ONLY

A life of
The Reverend THEODORE BAYLEY HARDY V.C., D.S.O., M.C.
1863—1918
Vicar of Hutton Roof, Westmorland

by
David Raw

For Patricia Hastings Hardy and Michael Westropp, without whose help, support and generosity it would not have been possible

ISBN 0 948511 45 1

Typeset by Facsimile Typesetters,
Gatebeck, near Kendal, Cumbria.

Printed and Published by Frank Peters Publishing Ltd.,
Gatebeck, near Kendal, Cumbria.

Copies of illustrations credited to the Imperial War Museum may be purchased from
their Department of Photographs, Lambeth Road, London SE1 6HZ.
The Visitors' Room is open by appointment to the public during the week.

Introduction and Acknowledgements

The casual visitor to Carlisle Cathedral will most certainly notice the massive sandstone walls, the magnificent ceiling, and the exquisite Flemish carving of the Brougham Triptych.

Less obvious is a brass memorial tablet on the north wall to a man who had other reasons for knowing Flanders in intricate detail. It commemorates a man who would probably have preferred it not to be noticed. He was at one time a diffident schoolmaster and an unassuming country vicar. He was also the most decorated non-combatant in the First World War: decorations won not in hot blood and anger, but in cool tenacious courage. He was to die only a few days before the Armistice.

The author's first knowledge of Theodore Bayley Hardy was a casual sight of that memorial tablet. It set off an urge to know more about this unknown hero which has culminated in the writing of this biography.

It is a story of incredible heroism that should not be forgotten. In today's world, where selfishness and individual greed dominate, it is a story of comradeship and unselfishness that ought to give us pause for thought. Above all, it is one man's Christian witness which even the most sceptical agnostic or strident atheist must respect.

*   *   *   *   *

One of the delights of writing this book has been to meet people who had connections with Theodore Hardy, or were able to help by providing source material and information. In particular, I would like to thank his grand-daughter Patricia Hardy for her hospitality and help in providing original material. A great debt is also owed to Canon Michael Westropp for his support, enthusiasm and generosity. It was a pleasure to meet and interview ex-Private James Watson of the 8th Lincolns. The Bishop of Penrith has been especially helpful in many ways, particularly with the Chapter on Hardy's New Testament.

Thanks are also due to Colonel Bailey and Captain Smith of the Lincolnshire Regiment (now, alas, the Royal Anglian Regiment). The Headmasters of Bentham Grammar School and Nottingham High School, and their staff, have provided valuable information as have the secretaries to the Bishop of Carlisle and Bishop of Southwell. The Local Studies Departments of Nottingham Public Library and Exeter Public Library have both been most helpful. I would especially thank Mr. Willis and Miss Fish of the Imperial War Museum who have taken a great deal of trouble on my behalf.

I am grateful to the Imperial War Museum for permission to reproduce photographs held in their collection.

I am also grateful to the various authors and their publishers who have allowed me to quote from their works.

One person it is now too late to thank, although she provided the central core of source material upon which this book has been built. In 1919, Hardy's sister-in-law Mary published a memoir, 'Hardy V. C. ', which included letters sent to her from men who had served with him in France. She wrote that, one day, she hoped a fuller account would be written of her brother-in-law's exploits. I hope that in some measure this book now answers her hope and that she would have been pleased with it.

Finally, I would thank Barbara Thomas for typing much of the manuscript, and also my family for their moral support and for putting up with a most untidy study littered with countless bits of paper.

David Raw,
Penrith, February, 1988.

"IT'S ONLY ME"

A life of
The Reverend THEODORE BAYLEY HARDY V.C., D.S.O., M.C.
1863—1918
Vicar of Hutton Roof, Westmorland

'After this it was noised abroad that Mr. Valiant-for-truth was taken with a
summons by the same post as the other, and had this for a token that the
summons was true, that his pitcher was broken at the fountain. When he
understood it he called for his friends, and told them of it. Then said he, I am
going to my Father's; and though with great difficulty I am got hither, yet
now I do not repent me of all the trouble I have been at to arrive where I am.
My sword I give to him that shall succeed me in my pilgrimage, and my
courage and skill to him that can get it. My marks and scars I carry with me,
to be a witness for me that I have fought His battles who now will be my
rewarder. When the day that he must go hence was come, many
accompanied him to the river side, into which as he went he said, "Death,
where is thy sting?" And as he went down deeper, he said, "Grave, where is
thy victory?" So he passed over, and all the trumpets sounded for him on the
other side.'

Mr. Valiant-for-truth crosses the river,

Pilgrim's Progress — John Bunyan

TAKEN WITH A SUMMONS

5.00 a.m., 11th October, 1918, River Selle, Briastres.

They knew he would come. He always did. Every night, you could count on it. Sometimes he had come from in front of them, from 'No Man's Land'. He had even been shot at by some of them when their nerves were twitching. Sometimes he brought a wounded man on his back, sometimes a body.

'It's only me, boys', he would say. 'There's nothing to be afraid of. He won't hurt you. Help me to bury him and then I'll read the burial service. You can join in if you wish.'

Tonight, though, he had come from behind them with a team of Lewis Gunners and stretcher bearers. He had scrambled down the bank and crossed the plank bridge just finished by the Engineers over the River Selle. All he brought tonight was cigarettes and the comfort of his presence.

He didn't need to say much. It was enough just to be with them. He asked if they had any letters he could take back. They spoke in whispers because the enemy was close. It couldn't last much longer they said. They had advanced thirty miles in the last month. Could this Christmas be the first one of peace in over four years?

A few birds sounded the coming dawn. He had to go he said.

Minutes later they heard a shot as he crossed the plank bridge. Seventy years later Jimmy Watson can still remember him saying, 'I've been hit. I'm sorry to be a nuisance'. Machine gun fire broke out all round the bridge and the advance platoons.

It was 11th October, 1918, exactly one month before the Armistice. The 8th Lincolns and 8th Somersets were to see only eight more days of action. A week later, their padre, Theodore Bayley Hardy, V.C., D.S.O., M.C., died of his wounds in Rouen. His daughter Elizabeth, a V.A.D. Nurse, wrote to thank the stretcher bearers for bringing him in under fire. "Yes", they wrote back, "it was difficult, but we would go through Hell itself for our dear old padre".

HIS FIRST AVOWED INTENT . . . . .

On the 20th October, 1863 a son was born to George and Sarah Hardy at Barnfield House in the Southernhay district of Exeter. They christened him Theodore Bayley Hardy.

The new baby was born into a large family of half-brothers from his mother's first marriage, and a full brother, Ernest. Sarah was twice widowed young. George Hardy, a commercial traveller, was to die in 1866 when Theodore was only three.

Theodore's mother was clearly an able and enterprising lady. In Morris's Directory of Devonshire for 1870 she is listed as having 'a select preparatory school for young gentlemen'. No doubt the school had helped her to survive financially when she had been widowed, and it allowed a more comfortable existence for her large family in a most respectable part of the city. Mary Hardy remembered a large Victorian house with tall windows and shallow staircases. It later became the Exeter Y.M.C.A.

Theodore and Ernest were educated by their mother until the age of about nine or ten. They then went as boarders to the City of London School. The school had an ancient foundation (1442), but it had expanded along with other public schools as the new aspiring Victorian middle class sought opportunities for their sons.[1]

The influence of Arnold at Rugby and Thring at Uppingham was felt in other public schools, and one can trace their impact on the young Hardy. From Arnold came the idea of the school as a community of Christian gentlemen; from Thring the value of games and physical education coupled with an appreciation of music. The basis of all public school education was still the classics, but history, modern languages, mathematics and even science were entering the curriculum. Religion, and the school chapel, was a central part of school life.

There is some evidence that Theodore Hardy missed family life at Exeter, and looked forward eagerly to the holidays. Yet he was well liked and successful, becoming captain of the school rowing club. By strange co-incidence the rowing club secretary was C.E. Montague, who was to write a bitter indictment of the First War, **Disenchantment,** which included critical remarks about the chaplains.[2] He specifically excluded Hardy from his general criticism of others.

As Theodore Hardy grew to manhood, his sister-in-law tells us that 'London's boundless possibilities for happiness, or unhappiness, oppressed him'. She also tells how, for him, music had 'a strange analogy to certain facts in our spiritual life. He found himself led into deep places by the world of sound'.[3] It became his habit to attend the afternoon service in Westminster Abbey every Sunday.

Theodore went on to London University, combining his studies with teaching work, whilst Ernest entered Queens University, Belfast, and like Theodore, in time was ordained a priest of the Church of England. Both brothers were to have Irish brides. Ernest's future wife, Mary, remembered Theodore at a dance in Ireland at the age of twenty-one:

'He was a man with the head of a scholar and the eyes of a poet. I remember being asked: "Who is that distinguished-looking young man standing in the corner?".'[4]

It was in Belfast that the young Hardy was to meet Florence Elizabeth Hastings. It was a love match. She dazzled him and yet she needed his quiet strength:

'She flashed about with her striking beauty and her wit in a sort of luminous mist. She was a brilliant talker, with a power of drawing in a scene or a personality in a few swift lines, yet without malice or uncharitableness. She was somewhat unconventional, far from being that curious combination of dullness and energy that the Church of England demands in a parson's wife.'[5]

Her father was a freelance architect in Belfast, and the Hastings were known as a clever and literary family. Theodore and Florence were to marry in September, 1888 at the Great Victoria Street Baptist Meeting House.

* * * * *

The young couple were to return to London where Hardy completed his studies and graduated as a Bachelor of Arts in 1889.

Money was not plentiful, a situation that was to remain with him for the rest of his life. Two children, Elizabeth and William, soon appeared. The question of a career had to be dealt with. After two years teaching in London, he applied for the post of Form Master to the Upper Second at Nottingham High School. His application was successful and sixteen happy years were to follow.

Nottingham High School, like the City of London School, was an ancient foundation but it too had expanded and grown in response to Victorian prosperity to provide an education for the sons of Nottingham's manufacturers and shopkeepers. The areas Hardy was required to teach provide a fascinating glimpse of what that education was. The Upper Second curriculum consisted of the following:

Sections of St. Luke and St. Matthew's Gospel
The Children's Treasury of English Song
History between 1603 and 1660
The Geography of Scotland and Ireland
English Analysis of Simple Sentences
French from the Chardenal French Course
Latin from Dr. Abbott's Via Latina
Arithmetic — Stocks and Shares — Problems of Area and Proportional Parts
Algebra — Factors — Simple Equations — Easy Problems
Geometry
Euclid — Examples 1-26[6]

It is interesting to note the lack of science and technical subjects — an omission not to be found in Germany or the United States.

Hardy was always keen on physical exercise and games (throughout his life he followed the public school habit of a daily cold bath). His keenness, however, was let down by poor eyesight. He regularly played for the school cricket team, but in sixteen years he failed to score a single run. [7]

The Hardy family in September, 1905.
The photograph was taken at Thurlby Vicarage, Lincolnshire.
It is not certain what the occasion was, although it may be that Hardy was acting as a holiday locum.

One of Nottingham's most famous sons, the novelist and poet D.H. Lawrence, had Hardy as a form master. It is strange that Lawrence attempted to cover up his rather middle class education in the auto-biographical novel *'Sons and Lovers';* perhaps it did not fit his image of the working class intellectual, although it certainly fits his mother's ambition for 'Paul Morel' to move up to a higher station in life.

Lawrence's biographer recalls an obsession with death, and a strange correspondence with his brother about skeletons and coffins. [8] This obsession led to a clash with his Form Master.

Hardy noticed that Lawrence was not attending to a lesson and seemed pre-occupied with the contents of his desk. The Form Master lifted the desk to discover Lawrence playing with a macabre set of toys: little skeletons, gibbets and coffins. Lawrence apparently took to his heels and ran off. The boy was later to seek his revenge by firing a paper pellet at Hardy when the latter was writing on the blackboard. Such was the meeting between England's most decorated non-combatant and one of her greatest novelists. [9] It is an odd quirk that twenty years later Hardy and his comrades were being shot at on the Western Front by the 'Red Baron' von Richthofen, whilst Lawrence was living in Mexico with Frieda, a relative of the German Air Ace.

In 1965, publicity about Hardy's medals brought an affectionate memory of his old Form Master from a former pupil, A.W. Adams: 'He was a very friendly type' . . . but 'He was a shortish man and the last person you would expect to win a V.C.' [10]

* * * * *

On the 18th December, 1898, at the age of thirty-five, Theodore Hardy was ordained a Deacon in the Church of England in Southwell Minster.

He had contemplated this step for ten years but had held back because he was not convinced on certain points of the Church's dogma. He could not accept the damnatory

4

clauses of the Athanasian Creed. At Nottingham High School he had met the Bishop of Southwell, George Riddings, and they soon developed a close accord. It was largely through many discussions with Bishop Riddings, that he had at last felt able to take the step to ordination. [11]

He was licensed as a curate at the village of Burton Joyce, a five-mile bicycle ride away. He helped with services on a Sunday and continued with his teaching career through the week.

A year after he became a Deacon, he took the final step and was ordained as Priest in St. George's Church, Nottingham. He stayed at Burton Joyce for three years, before moving to a more conveniently placed curacy at New Basford near to the High School.

His teaching career, too, was developing. He moved on to become a Third Form Master in 1902, and in 1905 he was promoted to become Joint Master of the new Modern Sixth.

Then in 1907, an advertisement caught his attention for a new Headmaster at Bentham Grammar School on the Yorkshire-Lancashire border near Lancaster.

[1] The City of London School had moved to a new site in Cheapside in the City in 1834, and moved again as it expanded to Victoria Embankment in 1883. The School had, and still has, strong musical traditions with a link with the Choir of the Chapel Royal. It was administered by the City Corporation.

[2] Montague went on to achieve fame on the *Manchester Guardian*. In *Disenchantment* appeared a chapter 'The Sheep That Were Not Fed', highly critical of the Chaplains. However, there was an exception:

> 'There was the hero and saint, T.B. Hardy, to whom a consuming passion of human brotherhood brought, as well as rarer things, the M.C., the D.S.O., the V.C., the unaccepted invitation of the King to come home as one of his own Chaplains and live, and then the death which everyone had seen to be certain.'

[3] Mary Hardy, *'Hardy V.C.'*, Skeffington, 1919.

[4] Ibid.

[5] Ibid.

[6] Letter to author from Dr. D.T. Witcombe, Headmaster of Nottingham High School, 15th September, 1987.

[7] Ibid.

[8] Keith Sagar, *The Life of D.H. Lawrence,* p.23, Eyre Methuen, London, 1980. Lawrence was the first boy from Eastwood to win one of the new £12 County Council Scholarships to the High School. It is very likely that he would be conscious of a social gap with the middle class fee payers.

He did, in fact, perform well at school, being top of his form in 1900 and winning a mathematics prize. His school report, despite the incident with Hardy, described his diligence and conduct as 'very good'. (Sagar, op. cit. p.21).

[9] *Nottingham Guardian Journal,* 25th September, 1965. Publicity about Hardy's medals being put on permanent loan to the Chaplains Department Museum prompted a letter from a former pupil, Mr. A.W. Adams. Another version exists in which Lawrence was supposed to have fired a pistol at Hardy and shattered the blackboard. It is difficult to accept this version (sent by another former pupil to the *Daily Telegraph* on 18th September, 1965) because it amounts to criminality and there is no record of disciplinary action against Lawrence.

[10] Ibid.

[11] Mary Hardy, op. cit.

Additional information supplied by the Secretary to the Bishop of Southwell.

HEADMASTER AND PRIEST

'He who would valiant be . . . 'gainst all disaster.'

The village of Bentham lies on the western edge of the Pennines in the valley of the River Wenning. The bulk of Ingleborough lies five miles to the north east and the ancient City of Lancaster is fifteen miles to the west.

The Grammar School had been established in 1726, and following a major re-organisation in 1877, it now supplied secondary education for about forty boys on a fee-paying basis. The teaching staff consisted of the Headmaster and one assistant master. The Head's wife was expected to take an interest in the boarders and a full part in the running of the school. The Head's salary was £120 a year, as it had been since 1876, although accommodation was provided for the Headmaster and his family. Most of the pupils were the sons of farmers and tradespeople.

In 1907, the previous Head decided to retire. There were 101 applicants for the post. Theodore Hardy was appointed. It may have helped that he had taught the son of the retiring Head at Nottingham High School.

Apart from the obvious attraction of becoming master of his own school, there were other factors in Hardy's wish to obtain the post. He loved the countryside and the opportunities it gave for fell walking and cycling. Bentham was also conveniently placed for the boat from Heysham to Northern Ireland, bringing contact with Florence's family much closer. He, in turn, was welcomed by the local clergy who could use him as a locum tenens.

Hardy threw himself into his new job, and was soon appreciated.

> 'Mr. Hardy won the admiration of all pupils, parents and friends by his whole-hearted enthusiasm in his work, his charming manly virtues, his purity and simplicity of character.' [1]

The official History of Bentham Grammar School states that '(Hardy) believed in hard work and hard play and set the standard himself'. He was first to take the plunge into the river when a new swimming club was launched. He was to stress the health of the locality in the School Prospectus, and set up a gymnasium in the school. He underpinned this emphasis on healthy living with his own practice of being teetotal and a vegetarian.

His habit of travelling everywhere by bicycle sometimes ended in hilarity as far as the pupils were concerned. His poor eyesight meant that he kept falling off his bike, and he would frequently appear at breakfast with a black eye after running into a gate. Yet their hilarity was based on genuine affection for the man.

The school offered a broad curriculum going beyond the traditional academic subjects. Hardy's predecessor, John Llewellyn, had wisely introduced an element of science with an agricultural slant and book-keeping. Hardy's love of music added a further dimension to the school.

The Reverend T. B. Hardy, Headmaster, and boys of Bentham Grammar School, circa 1908.

The Headmaster's house, Bentham Grammar School.

The School-room, Bentham Grammar School, as Hardy would have known it. This was the only classroom in Hardy's time. The photograph was taken in the 1920's, by which time it had become known as 'Hardy Hall' in remembrance of the former headmaster.

All was going well. The Hardys were liked and respected by both the school and the village. The boarders had a special affection for the lively and amusing Mrs. Hardy . . . when disaster struck . . . Florence was found to be seriously ill and was given only a short time to live in the Summer of 1913.

This was a devastating blow for the whole family. They were a close and unusually loving family. William was by now studying to be a doctor at Queens University at Belfast, whilst Elizabeth was at London University. Both desperately wanted to be at home with their mother, and a letter from Theodore to William at this time talks of a tearful farewell on the Bentham Road.

It was clearly impossible for Florence to carry on her work at the school. Hardy also felt the need to be with her and to nurse her through her illness. He submitted his resignation to the Governors, and it was arranged that he should take over the living of the parish of Hutton Roof as Priest-in-Charge. [2]

* * * * *

Hutton Roof was, and is, a scattered rural community near Kirkby Lonsdale at the Southern end of Westmorland (now Cumbria). It is an area of rolling hills and narrow country lanes. The small squat church nestles under the shadow of the limestone Hutton Roof Craggs. Bentham lies across the River Lune ten miles to the south west, but Ingleborough Hill still dominates the landscape. The people have a slow regular way of life, a way of life usually marked with courtesy and consideration for others. Here the Hardys were to make their new home. Their new parishioners made them welcome.

Theodore Hardy's cousin, Miss Bessie Hardy, came up from Devon to help them settle in. She has left a graphic description of their new home:

> 'The scenery all the way was magnificent — we turned up a little lane some distance from the main entrance to the Vicarage, just at the foot of the Cragg, crossed a hayfield, and then through a little wicket, at the end of a terrace and avenue of firs, beeches, sycamores and chestnuts; rose-beds were dotted along a grass walk just below the terrace; great moss-grown boulders jutted out at intervals, and half way along the terrace were an old archway and mossy steps leading down to the rose-beds; a few yards further and we came to the conservatory, through which we entered the south side of the Vicarage into the dining-room. Looking through the front window the view was indeed a transformation — now we were gazing on the majestic grandeur of Ingleborough.' [3]

But despite this beauty it was a house of sadness. In June, 1914 on a Sunday morning, Theodore went across to the church to pray. When he returned William told him that Florence had died. They buried her in Hutton Roof Church Yard.

* * * * *

In the same month, a shot rang out in Sarajevo which was to change the history of the world. Within five short weeks, the assassination of the Arch-Duke and Duchess of Austria was to lead to a World War which would change, and end, the lives of millions.

In Hutton Roof, life had to carry on. Hardy's answer to his sorrow was predictable, he threw himself into his work. He would also go for long walks on the Cragg by himself, and in a letter to Mary Hardy, he told of how he had 'met consolation, even refreshment on the way'. [4] His faith had survived the test.

Hutton Roof Vicarage.
'The Vicarage was literally open house; very seldom were the doors locked; all visitors were hospitably welcomed —
tramps were given a good meal and a hot pot of tea. '

Bessie Hardy

Hutton Roof Vicarage,
Kirkby Lonsdale.
27 - viii - 15.

Dear Corporal Wilson,

Having heard from your father that you have been some time at the Front, I am writing to congratulate you on taking part in the splendid work that is being done by our army abroad. I hope that you may come back safe and sound but still more that you may be enabled to keep up to the very high standard of duty set by your Comrades. I know that you have things to face which most of us could hardly have imagined, ~~a~~ ~~strain on the nerves~~ but if you are going at them in the spirit in which you went at your scout work, I am sure you will be able to answer as a British soldier should any call that is made on you. You won't forget, I think, from Whom the strength comes. — I could enter well into your father's feelings of pride and anxiety, because my son is at the Front too: he is in the R. A. M. C. and is at present very near the Dardanelles, working in a "stationary" hospital and field ambulances.

I should like very much, a short letter telling me something about your experiences, as far as the censor will allow: — but I don't want you to bother to write if you are busy — if — like a good many people — you dislike letter-writing: — just send me a post-card to say you have had this and — I hope — a little joy parcel I am getting Thexton to send.

— — wishing you God speed —

I am, Yours sincerely,

T. B. Hardy.

In October, cousin Bessie Hardy came to be his housekeeper when Elizabeth went back to university. She again gives a vivid description of life at Hutton Roof Vicarage:

'The Vicarage was literally open house; very seldom were the doors locked; all visitors were hospitably welcomed — tramps were given a good meal and a hot pot of tea; on one occasion I remember going for a conveyance so that a poor woman could be driven to the nearest workhouse, where she was trying to walk under great difficulties, her feet being badly ulcerated; after rest and a good dinner, she and her husband were driven off, amidst grateful thanks to his "Riverence".'

She goes on to describe how he adopted a gun-shy dog which would otherwise have been put down. On one occasion a monster rat escaped from the cat into the drawing room. Hardy opened the window and said, 'Let it get free, it has fought for its life'.

It was at this time he met a young man who was to develop into a larger than life country character in Kirkby Lonsdale, the Blacksmith, Jonty Wilson. Jonty has been the subject of a biography by Dalesman Books. It became the custom in later years for Jonty to give the valediction 'We Will Remember Them' in Kirkby Lonsdale Church on Remembrance Sunday. He would often recall Theodore Hardy:

'As a young man I acted as Assistant Scoutmaster to the 1st Kirkby Lonsdale Troop of Boy Scouts. We had a permanent camp on Hutton Roof Craggs and during the summer months spent many happy week-ends there. That is how I first met Mr. Hardy and a friendship developed which lasted until his death in Rouen in 1918. Often on week-day nights I would go to Hutton Roof and call at the Vicarage for Mr. Hardy. We would creep up the Cragg in the dusk to spend nights in the camp. Lovely scented nights they were, with the smell of bracken and juniper, the steep hillsides dotted with glow-worms and the night-jar "jerring" from the rocky out-crops on the tops.' [6]

When the war came Jonty joined as a volunteer with the Westmorland and Cumberland Yeomanry. A correspondence continued between them until Hardy's death. One of those letters to Jonty in August, 1915 is reproduced in this book. It indicates Hardy's attitude to the war, and also his wish to know what is going on. It still has the black band of mourning over twelve months after Florence's death. Jonty Wilson was to attend Theodore Hardy's funeral just over three years later.

Two other letters written by Theodore Hardy at this time survive. Both were to William who had graduated as a doctor in March, 1915. The letters are worth reproducing in full because they reveal Hardy's feelings about his wife's death, his warmth and love for his children, his generosity despite his lack of wealth, and his willingness (despite his poor sight) to undertake a fifteen mile cycle ride in the middle of the night before a Sunday service.

Hutton Roof Vicarage
March 23rd 1915

Dear Will,

I can't go to bed without writing my congratulations although I hope you have started for home before this letter reaches Belfast. It is splendid to think that you have really done it and we are sure that Mother knows this and is glad with us — to whom, under God, you chiefly owe it. I must say also that I am very very proud of you, Will, for I know how real the difficulties you have had and the temptations to steer clear of. I don't think you will ever forget those Goodbyes in the road at Bentham. As to difficulties, on the score of health alone no one could have blamed you at all if you had taken at least a year longer, and many would have taken more than that.

Well, now you have got the degree, thank God for that, a real step in life, up to a position of power for good, and I pray God that you always use it with a sense of your responsibility to Him. I am sure that Mother is praying with me that your life as a man may be worthy, and in thanking Him for the past. I hope you have sent a telegram to Elizabeth, but I shall send one tomorrow when I send yours — to make sure. With much love and heartiest congratulations from your affectionate and proud Father.

Twenty-four hours later we have another letter — in a much lighter vein.
Theodore Hardy had decided to go to Belfast for the graduation ceremony.

Hutton Roof
24.3.15

Dear Doctor,

I am sorry I cannot reply to your letter, which came by the morning post, sooner than by tomorrow morning, but I suppose it isn't necessary to telegraph.

I have made out with some searching of timetables that I can get over for Saturday, and shall be very glad indeed to come. I didn't think the presentation for degrees would be so soon. Please thank Aunt Mary for asking me to stay, but I shall come by the Saturday morning Heysham boat and go back by Stranraer: you know I like railway travelling and I hope to get a good sleep on the train and in the Heysham boat if the weather is good. I can get back to Carnforth by 1.30 a.m. Sunday and shall leave my bicycle there going. Will you come back with me or have you made other plans? I should be very glad if you did, but it seems a pity to hurry away, if there is anything you would like to do, and I shouldn't see much of you on Sunday.

Elsie Peck is staying over Sunday but it isn't sure whether Elizabeth will be able to come or not, because of a lecture that may be given.

I have written this cheque for £12 — Mind this is all my business, it is only once in my lifetime I have a son's medical degrees to pay for and I enjoy it — This leaves me a fair balance (the words 'This doesn't overdraw by a good deal' are crossed out) *and I have an instalment of £20 odd, I think, coming on April 5th.*

I went into Mathews, after sending my telegram to you this morning. They were very nice and interested and complimentary to you. I won't write more now as I hope I shall be seeing you soon.

With love and congratulations (once more) *Your affectionate Father.*[7]

Shortly after William graduated he volunteered to join the Army as a doctor. He was sent out to the Dardanelles within a matter of weeks.

* * * * *

Theodore Hardy, too, even at the age of fifty-one, felt that he should be involved in the war. Time after time he applied to the Chaplaincy Department only to be told that they had a waiting list hundreds long of men much younger than himself.

He seriously thought of going not as a Chaplain, but as a volunteer stretcher bearer. He attended an Ambulance Class in Kirkby Lonsdale and successfully passed the examination.

Hardy was not a man to be deflected, and finally his persistence paid off. He was called for the interview in the Summer of 1916, and to his great delight was accepted. The Battle of the Somme had not only produced a shortage of troops, it had produced a shortage of Chaplains as well.

His rank was to be that of a Captain. His rank as a Chaplain cannot but produce a hint of irony — it was Temporary Chaplain, 4th Class.

[1] James Bibby, *A History of Bentham,* 1931.
    Much of the information in this section is derived form *The History of Bentham Grammar School, 1726 - 1976,* Huddleston, Wilson and Warbrick, 1976. Published by Titus Wilson of Kendal.
[2] The living of Hutton Roof was in the gift of the Vicar of Kirkby Lonsdale. It provided an income of £165 per annum.
    The parish had a population of 245 in the 1901 Census. There was a school, and also a small Methodist chapel. The church (dedicated to St. John) had been rebuilt in 1880. The small neighbouring parish of Lupton was included in Hardy's care.
[3] Mary Hardy, op. cit.
[4] Ibid.
[5] Ibid.
[6] Jonty Wilson, Notes for Remembrance Sunday, in possession of his daughter, Mrs. Cox. Jonty Wilson was the subject of a biography *A Cumbrian Blacksmith* published by Dalesman Books in 1978.
[7] Letters in possession of Miss Patricia Hastings Hardy.

TO BE A PADRE

'There's no discouragement, shall make him once relent . . .'

By the end of August, 1916, the new Temporary Chaplain 4th Class was kitted out, given a Captain's uniform with the distinctive Maltese Cross badge, and a travel warrant from Charing Cross via Folkestone and Boulogne to France. His destination was the huge base camp of Etaples set amongst the sand dunes on the Channel coast.

Etaples must have seemed a bewildering contrast to the peace and tranquillity of Hutton Roof in rural Westmorland. At its height, well over one hundred thousand men were accommodated and put through intensive training for the front. Bugles would ring out for reveille at 5.30 a.m. summer and winter alike, and the base would resound to the shouts and yells of the 'Canary' Instructors in the dreaded Bull Ring training ground set amongst the sand dunes. It was a desolate and hated place, destined to be the scene of a major mutiny in September, 1917, which threatened to bring the Passchendaele offensive grinding to a halt. [1]

The poet Wilfred Owen described Etaples in a letter home:

'I lay awake in a windy tent in the middle of a vast, dreadful encampment. It seemed neither France nor England, but a kind of paddock where the beasts are kept a few days before the shambles. I heard the revelling of the Scotch troops, who are now dead, and who knew they would be dead.

I thought of the very strange look on all faces in that camp; an incomprehensible look, which a man will never see in England; nor can it be seen in any battle. But only in Etaples.

It was not despair, or terror, it was more terrible than terror, for it was a blindfold look, and without expression, like a dead rabbit's.' [2]

When Theodore Hardy arrived the base was humming with activity as new units were sent up to take part in the second month of the great and dreadful offensive on the Somme. One hundred trains a day would take re-inforcements up to the line and bring back the dying and the wounded. Between 1st July and 16th November, 1916, British losses on the Somme would total nearly 420,000.

He was posted to two Infantry Base Depots in the Reinforcement Area of Etaples. There was a continual turnover of men, and it must have been difficult to make more than the merest contact with any individual before they were gone.

Here, also, he would have to come to terms with exactly what his role as an Army Chaplain was to be. Having at long last won the battle of admission into the Chaplaincy, he was to show the same persistence in pressing for what he really wanted, a posting to the front line. The Assistant Chaplain General, the Reverend Douglas Carey, was to write of the interview,

'Normally one hesitated to recommend a Chaplain of over fifty years of age for work in the line, but I have been intensely glad ever since that I had the common sense to see that it was with no ordinary mortal that I had to deal on this occasion. He had done good work during his time with me; he told me that he had always kept fit, had done regular physical exercises, and had been accustomed to a cold bath daily all the year round. He also stated that he was a widower, that both his children were grown up, and that he had no fear of death. His appeal was irresistible. I recommended his case to the Deputy Chaplain General, and, to his joy, my recommendation was acted upon.' [3]

Theodore Hardy knew with instinctive certainty that the front line was the place where he ought to be. When he got there he was to demonstrate by action as much as by words what that certainty meant.

Knowing what to do and getting on with it, marked him out as different from a great many other Chaplains who, although well intentioned, came in for severe criticism both during and after the war.

Alan Lloyd in his book, *The War in the Trenches* notes that 'first-hand accounts of trench warfare suggest a conspicuous absence of padres in the forward lines — a curious omission when, as Bishop W.C. Wand (himself a World War I chaplain) noted later, the war was making even the most careless face the issues of life and death; and when the fundamental questions of religion and philosophy had to be tackled afresh.' [4]

Siegfried Sassoon was to write, after he was wounded at Arras:

'The Dressing Station was a small underground place crowded with groaning wounded. Two doctors were doing what they could for men who had paid a heavy price for their freedom. My egocentricity diminished among all that agony. I remember listening to an emotional padre who was painfully aware that he could do nothing except stand about and feel sympathetic. The consolations of the Church of England weren't much in demand at an Advance Dressing Station.' [5]

Over the years, one must feel sympathy for the misery and sadness of that inadequate cleric. Yet as we will see, standing around with wringing hands was not what Theodore Hardy became known for.

Perhaps the most devastating criticism of the Chaplains came from C.E. Montague in the Chapter, 'The Sheep that Were Not Fed' in his book *Disenchantment* written soon after the war:

'There were all sorts and conditions of men among them (the chaplains), some good; some bad, like the chaplain drunk at dinner in Gobert's restaurant in Amiens on the evening of one of the bloodiest days of the first battle of the Somme. There was the man, who urged by national comradeship, would have been a soldier but that his bishop banned it: to be an army chaplain was the next best thing. There was the man, who, urged by a different instinct, felt irresistibly that at that moment the war was the central thing in the whole world and that it was unbearable not to be at the centre of things. And there was, in great force, the large, healthy, pleasant young curate ... He abounded so much that whenever now one hears the words "Army Chaplain" his large genial image springs up of itself in the mind.'

Montague goes on to conclude that, consciously or unconsciously, men at the front acquired a receptiveness to spiritual values which presented the churches with a unique opportunity. Yet:

> 'Nobody used it: the tide in the affairs of churches flowed its best, but no church came to take it. Instead, as if chance had planned a kind of satiric practical epigram, came the brigade chaplain. As soon as his genial bulk hove in sight, and his cheery robustious chaff began blowing about, the shy and uncouth muse of our savage theology unfolded her wings and flew away. Once more the talk was all footer and rations and scragging the Kaiser.' [6]

There could also be a tragic sectarian narrowness which brought heartbreaking grief. A devout Scottish soldier serving in an English Regiment wrote home from the front to say that he was about to take part in an attack, but that he had been refused communion by the Anglican Padre. The soldier was killed in the attack. [7]

Yet it is too easy and simplistic to criticise men finding themselves facing a situation so profoundly and horrifically different to the often small world of the pre-war Church. One must remember, too, that social differences were sharp and that there was bound to be a communication gap between a largely middle-class clergy and the other ranks of the British Army. It is not surprising that many were found wanting.

A pre-war survey in the City of York showed that only twenty-eight per cent of the population were church goers, and that of this group the vast majority were middle class with women outnumbering men. [8]

Robert Graves has asserted that, 'Hardly one soldier in a hundred was inspired by religious feeling of even the crudest kind.' Whilst this may be an overstatement, John Baynes, an officer who made a study of morale on the Western Front, reckoned that one ranker in every two attached no importance to religion in the trenches, and yet:

> 'Many would laugh at religion one day and pray most sincerely the next, particularly if under heavy shell fire. My estimate is that forty per cent reacted in this way.' [9]

Bernard Martin, a Lieutenant in the 64th Foot, remembered being given his identity discs, which, despite the fact that he was a member of the Church of Scotland, had C. of E. stamped on them.

> 'Why do you put a chap's religion on the disc, sergeant?'
> He laughed. 'Precaution, sir, precaution. In war you never can tell.'
> 'Tell what?'
> 'Why, sir, if your number should happen to come up, you wouldn't want the chaplains to quarrel about who's to bury you.'
> 'I'm not really C. of E.,' I observed mildly.
>
> The sergeant said in the tone of a wise man talking to an inexperienced youth, 'You stick to C. of E., sir. You wouldn't want to be buried by the Pope, I'm sure.'

I laughed. 'I don't suppose it makes any difference.'

'Oh, it does make a difference, sir.' He spoke earnestly. 'It does. RCs go to Hell before they get to Heaven — that's official. RCs call it Purgatory. You're definitely better off as C. of E., sir.'

Martin again describes the climate of religious feeling when writing of a Church Parade.

'I don't know who ordered the church parades when we came out on Rest. During my first eight months we had ten, but only three in seven months of 1917. I liked these parades, they were simple, no rituals or theology, only hymns, a lesson read from the Bible and a short address by the Chaplain. (In the front line we had no religion — that is no church parades, no regular visits from our Chaplain.) The men were indifferent though most sang the hymns, probably to words other than those printed in the hymn books.' [10]

This was the challenge of horror, indifference and inadequacy that Theodore Hardy had to face when he heard he was to join the 8th Battalion of the Lincolnshire Regiment in early December 1916. Douglas Carey's response to a request for some tips was to introduce him to a fellow Chaplain just down from the line. It was to be a meeting of two of the most extraordinary men to have served in the war, and who between them more than redeemed the mistakes and inadequacies of others. Early in December, 1916 Theodore Hardy spent an hour meeting Geoffrey Studdert-Kennedy in the office of the Assistant Chaplain General at Etaples.

Both men were to get beyond the outward show of formal religion to penetrate a deeper communion of souls; the sense of brotherhood and comradeship which produced a bond between soldier and soldier, a true communion where men shouldered the burdens of their weaker mates, risked their lives to rescue a comrade, and would try to help the families of dead friends. Both men knew that to penetrate this brotherhood they had to be part of it.

[1] See Norman Gladden, *Ypres 1917* pp 26/27, Kimber 1967.
and also William Allison and John Fairley, *The Monocled Mutineer,* Quartet Books, 1979.
[2] *Wilfred Owen: Collected letters* pp 67/68, edited by H. Owen and J. Bell, London 1967.
[3] Letter from Rev. D.F. Carey to Mrs Mary Hardy, quoted in *Hardy V.C.* Skeffington, 1919.
[4] Alan Lloyd, *The War in the Trenches* pp 133/139, Hart-Davis MacGibbon, 1976.
[5] Siegfried Sasson, *Memoirs of an Infantry Officer,* Faber and Faber, 1965.
[6] C.E. Montague, *Disenchantment.*
[7] Private information to author.
[8] Quoted in Lloyd, op. cit.
[9] Lloyd, op. cit.
[10] Bernard Martin, *Poor Bloody Infantry,* John Murray, 1987.

A MEETING WITH WOODBINE WILLIE

'It isn't proved, you fool, it can't be proved.
How can you prove a victory before
It's won? How can you prove a man who leads
To be a leader worth the following,
Unless you follow to the death?'

Faith — Geoffrey Studdert-Kennedy.

Theodore Hardy and Geoffrey Studdert-Kennedy make a remarkable contrast, yet they warmed to one another immediately. Studdert-Kennedy was twenty years younger than Hardy, and had been a Chaplain for just over a year. Already he was becoming well known, and was on the brink of the enormous fame which was to follow and bestow upon him the name of 'Woodbine Willie.'

He combined the clownish pathos of Chaplin with the nervous eloquence and wit of Aneurin Bevan and the radical Irish forthrightness of Bob Geldof. His biographer describes the large bat-wing ears; the mouth giving an impression of being over large for its surroundings; but the most remarkable feature of his physical appearance was his eyes:

> 'They were very large, very brown; but also for some reason or other — quite extraordinarily sad. Many people have sad eyes in this world, and with reason. But here it seems were eyes reflecting deep within themselves a sadness more profound, more elemental than anything arising from the mere slings and arrows of outrageous fortune. Here were eyes, in fact, whose sadness seemed to be of another wordly dimension, as though the possessor of them had found God himself in tears.' [1]

He suffered dreadfully from asthma and yet rescued the wounded in gas attacks. He was to win the Military Cross at Messines Ridge in June, 1917. Like Hardy, he was to be appointed a Chaplain to the King.

At Etaples, despite the prevailing indifference to things religious, Studdert-Kennedy could pack a hall with tough Australians wanting to hear him speak. He could startle an audience into attention with the words, 'I know what you're thinking, here comes the bloody parson.' Masking the Celtic sadness was an outrageously amusing wit and humour. He wrote poetry of immense power.

When he arrived in France, he had told the Assistant Chaplain General that at one time he had been, 'a revolutionary agnostic socialist who used to stand on a tub and talk in public places in the Midlands'. His reward for disclosing this piece of information was to be sent to minister to the needs of the troops passing through the canteen of Rouen railway station on their way to the front. Here he would,

> 'stand on a box and announce to the crowds of soldiery that he was about to sing *Mother Machree* for the sons, *Little Grey Home in the West* for the husbands, *The Sunshine of your Smile* for the lovers. Afterwards he would offer to write home for them, and was

seen to be doing so, surrounded by a throng pressing in on him. And when the time came for them to go, he would be by the train as it pulled out until he was left, heavy with his thoughts, to watch its vanishing tail-light.' [2]

This man, who could reach the hearts and minds of so many otherwise indifferent, could also be grossly misunderstood, as when General Plumer, all red cheeks and white moustache, stormed out of a sermon and demanded his removal from the chaplaincy.

The Reverend Geoffrey Studdert-Kennedy, M.C.
1883 - 1929

"and Evangelist gave him one smile, and bid him God-Speed;
so he went on with haste".

Pilgrim's Progress — John Bunyan

Yet the great meetings, the clowning boxing matches with the champion Jimmy Driscoll, all these things and more, took second place to where Studdert-Kennedy wanted to be — at the front. And it was of the front that they talked.

In a letter to Mary Hardy, Geoffrey Studdert-Kennedy wrote of their meeting:

'I remember the conversation very well, and the memory has never left me. I would not have dared to hope that it could really have exercised an influence on Hardy's glorious life, and your letter makes me feel very glad and very small. I will describe the interview as I remember it.

I had come down from the line, to my great disappointment, having been recalled to preach the National Mission. I was sick as mud at being recalled, and full of longing to get back to work in the line about which I was enthusiastic. Mr. Carey told me of a wonderful man who was serving with him, and had specially applied to go up the line, although he really was too old. He said Mr. Hardy would like very much to talk with me before he went up, and get some "tips" about the work, and had asked him to arrange an interview. I was very glad to do what I could.

He came to me at Mr. Carey's office. I remember what struck me first was that he was not young and not strong. Then as I talked I began to feel quite honestly that this man was a kind of saint. I think it was his humility, and utter willingness to learn, and his eagerness for sacrifice that struck me — most of all his humility. He asked me to tell him what the best way of working up there was.

I said: "Live with the men. Go everywhere they go. Make up your mind that you will share all their risks, and more if you can do any good. You can take it that the best place for a Padre (provided he does not interfere with military operations) is where there is most danger of death. Our first job is to go beyond the men in self-sacrifice and reckless devotion. Don't be bamboozled into believing that your proper place is behind the line; it isn't. If you stay behind you might as well come down, you won't do a ha'porth of good. Your place is in the front. The line is the key to the whole business. Work in the front, and they will listen to you when they come out to rest, but if you only preach and teach behind, you are wasting time, the men won't pay the slightest attention to you. The men will forgive you anything but lack of courage and devotion; without that you are useless."

I remember walking up and down and saying this very fiercely, because I was full of it. He took it all so humbly and eagerly that I was ashamed of myself, and loved him. Then I said, "The Devil tries to get at you by telling you that you could really do no good in the line, and that you were more use alive than dead. It was the Devil and a lie — the more Padres died in battle doing Christ-like deeds, the better for the Church. Most of us will be more use dead than alive!"

I remember we both looked at one another when I blundered out with that odd speech, and laughed. Then he asked me about purely spiritual work, and the opportunities for it.

I said: "There is very little purely spiritual work, it is all muddled and mixed — but it is all spiritual. Take a box of fags in your haversack and a great deal of love in your heart, and go up to them, laugh with them, joke with them; you can pray with them sometimes, but pray for them always."

As we talked he got more enthusiastic. The programme appealed to him, and I loved him because it appealed, and I felt that he would do it all much better than I had ever been able to do, because he had the power that belongs to saints, and I was just such a beastly ordinary man.

I told him some yarns, and we both roared, laughing over them,

Then I was interrupted and had to go to a meeting. We shook hands, and I have never seen him since, but I loved him then, and I love him now. He is one of the best, and God must enjoy him tremendously. If I did influence him, it is just another proof of the queer instruments God can use to do jobs with, but I believe that, if he had never seen me or heard of me, he would inevitably have done what he did, because he was in his soul a hero and a saint.

P.S. — On reading this I find that Hardy says nothing — that was what he really did say; he just didn't speak much; he listened and was himself, and he looked pure, fine enthusiasm.' [3]

Although they never did meet again, there is no doubt (as we will see) that Studdert-Kennedy did indeed make a profound impression on Theodore Hardy. Hardy himself was to say as much when he answered a letter of congratulations from Douglas Carey upon the award of his V.C. over eighteen months later:

'Are you likely to meet or write to Studdert-Kennedy soon? If so, will you tell him that I have often wished I could thank him properly for that hour in your office which, more than almost any other in my life, has helped me in this work — you must admit that you can understand how I feel about these ribbons when I think of him!' [4]

A few days before Hardy went to join his new battalion, Carey saw him at the Chaplains' School in St. Omer. He was, noted Carey, supremely happy. To a member of his family, Hardy said at this time that all his previous life and work had been but a preparation, a leading up to his work as a Chaplain; all his life it would seem, he had been haunted by a sort of dream of some curious and great experience that was waiting for him. [5]

---

[1] William Purcell, *Woodbine Willie — a study of Geoffrey Studdert-Kennedy,* p.15, Mowbray 1962.
[2] Ibid. p.11.
[3] Mary Hardy, *Hardy V.C.* op. cit. Letter written by Geoffrey Studdert-Kennedy, pp 24/27.
[4] Letter written by T.B. Hardy to Rev. D.F. Carey, 24.7.1918.
[5] Mary Hardy, op. cit. p.23.

HIS MATE

There's a broken, battered village,
 Somewhere up behind the line,
There's a dug-out and a bunk there
 That I used to say were mine.

I remember how I reached them,
 Dripping wet and all forlorn,
In the dim and dreary twilight
 Of a weeping summer morn.

All that week I'd buried brothers,
 In one bitter battle slain,
In one grave I laid two hundred.
 God! What sorrow and what rain!

And that night I'd been in trenches,
 Seeking out the sodden dead,
And just dropping them in shell-holes,
 With a service swiftly said.

For the bullets rattled round me,
 But I couldn't leave them there,
Water-soaked in flooded shell-holes,
 Reft of common Christian prayer.

So I crawled round on my belly,
 And I listened to the roar
Of the guns that hammered Thiepval,
 Like big breakers on the shore.

Then there spoke a dripping sergeant,
 When the time was growing late,
'Would you please to bury this one,
 'Cause 'e used to be my mate?'

So we groped our way in darkness
 To a body lying there,
Just a blacker lump of blackness,
 With a red blotch on his hair.

Though we turned him gently over,
 Yet I still can hear the thud,
As the body fell face forward,
 And then settled in the mud.

We went down upon our faces,
 And I said the service through,
From 'I am the Resurrection'
 To the last, the great 'adieu'.

We stood up to give the Blessing,
 And commend him to the Lord,
When a sudden light shot soaring
 Silver swift and like a sword.

At a stroke it slew the darkness,
 Flashed its glory on the mud,
And I saw the sergeant staring
 At a crimson clot of blood.

There are many kinds of sorrow
 In this world of Love and Hate,
But there is no sterner sorrow
 Than a soldier's for his mate.

Geoffrey Studdert Kennedy

Geoffrey Studdert-Kennedy.

After the War

"I know thy works: behold, I have set before thee an open door, and no man can shut it: for thou hast a little strength, and hast kept my word, and hast not denied my name." (Revelation 3.8)

Marked by T.B. Hardy in his pocket New Testament, and carried by him throughout 1916-1918.

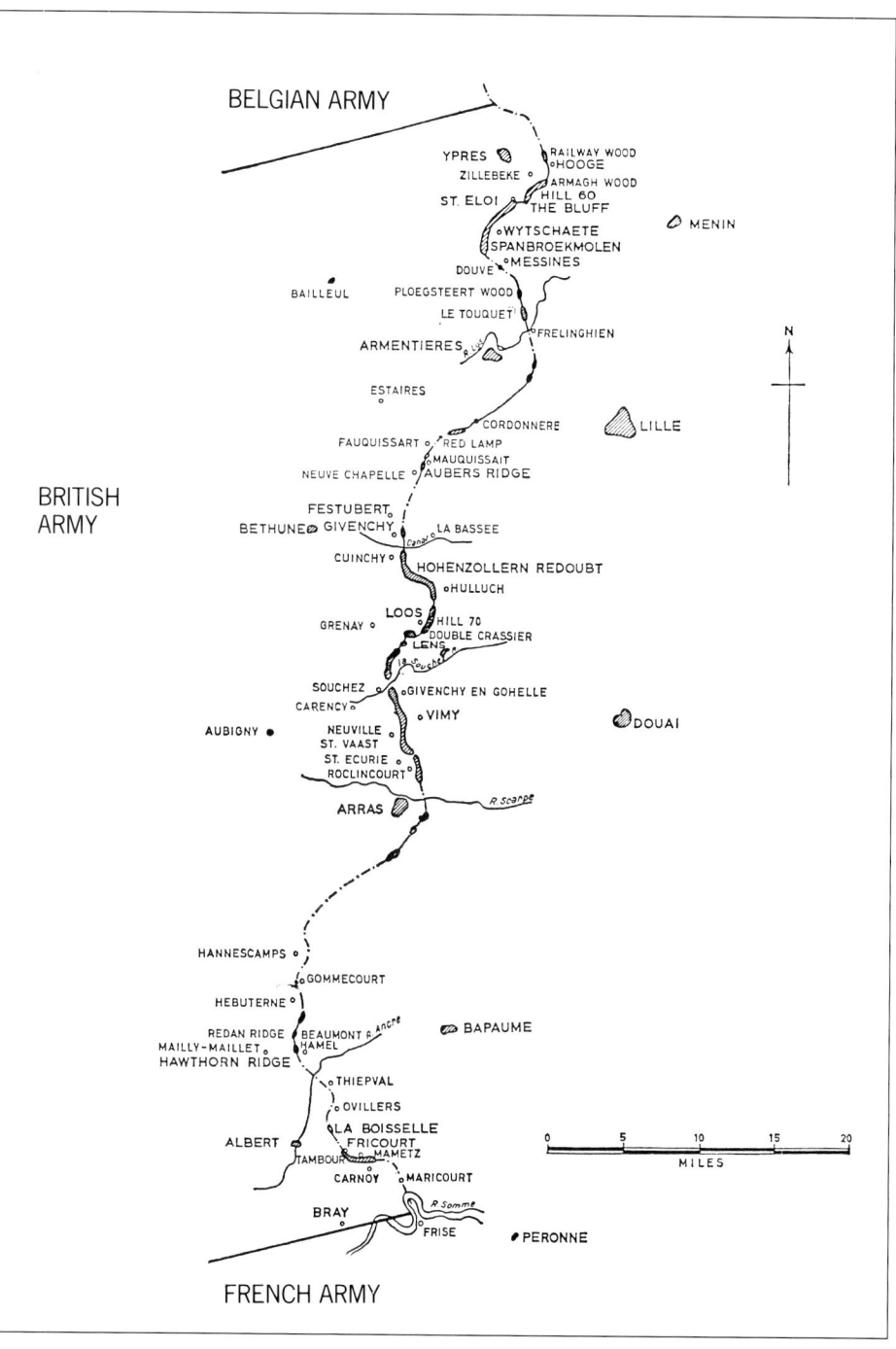

The British Sector of the Western Front, mid 1916 before the Somme.

26

COMMAND STRUCTURE OF THE BRITISH EXPEDITIONARY FORCE IN FRANCE: JANUARY, 1917

COMMANDER-IN-CHIEF, Field Marshal Sir Douglas Haig

1st ARMY   2nd ARMY   *3rd ARMY*   4th ARMY   5th ARMY
General Sir Edmund Allenby
General Sir Julian Byng (April, 1917)
Each Army was made up of 10 Divisions, with approximately 10,000 men in each Division:—

37th Division Commanded by a *Major-General*
Each Division usually consisted of three brigades.

63rd Infantry Brigade, Commanded by a *Lieutenant Colonel*
Each brigade consisted of four battalions (sometimes three in 1918)

8th Battalion, Lincolnshire Regiment   8th Somersets   10th Yorks & Lancs.   4th Middlesex
Each battalion consisted of 36 officers and 1,000 men
The battalion was commanded by a *Lieutenant Colonel*

The battalion was divided into four *Companies,* under a *Major or Captain* (240 men)

Each Company was divided into four *Platoons,* under a *Lieutenant and a Sergeant* (60 men)

Each Platoon was divided into four *Sections,* with a *Corporal and about 12 Privates*

Theodore Hardy was attached to the 8th Battalion, the Lincolnshire Regiment in December, 1916. He was soon to add the 8th Battalion of the Somersets to his care, a total of nearly two thousand men when at full strength.

The 8th Lincolns were part of the 63rd Infantry Brigade in the 37th Division.

In the Summer of 1917 they were transferred to the 2nd Army under Sir Herbert Plumer, but returned to the 3rd Army during the Spring of 1918.

THE WESTERN FRONT
1914–1918

MILES 0   20   40   60   80 MILES

Allied Line July 1, 1916 —————
(before Somme battles)

Allied Line March 21, 1918 ············
(Allied advances of 1916-17)

Armistice Line — — —

Theodore Hardy's War

T.B. Hardy arrived in France in August, 1916, spending the next four months in the base at Etaples, south of Boulogne. He arrived at the Front near Lens in December, 1916.

He transferred south to Arras at the end of March, 1917, before moving north to the Ypres salient at the end of June.

He was to stay in the Ypres area until the end of March, 1918. He then moved to Gommecourt ten miles to the north of Albert. He was to stay there until August, and then took part in the final Allied offensive until he was wounded to the east of Cambrai. He was taken to the Military Hospital in Rouen where he died on 18th October, 1918.

28

TO THE FRONT LINE

'He chose the Cross: that was his way henceforth. Now there's a glamour even about the Cross until you actually shoulder it, and then if there is any glamour at all, it is only other people who see it.'

Mary Hardy, sister-in-law of T. B. Hardy, 1919.

When Theodore Hardy joined the 8th Lincolns at Sarton in December, 1916, it was in the hardest winter on record since 1880/81. The military correspondent of *The Times* reported that the Household Cavalry infantry battalion had had heavy losses from frostbite.[1] Sir Douglas Haig, Commander-in-Chief of the British Armies, recorded 25 degrees of frost in his diary, and noted that at Boulogne the sands were all frozen as the tide went back.[2]

Hardy joined with a large draft of new recruits needed to replace heavy losses suffered during four and a half months of the dreadful Somme offensive. Between 1st July and 20th November, 1916, the battalion lost 40 officers and over 100 N.C.O.s: total casualties on the first day of the offensive (1st July) amounted to 251 — in the last week up to 20th November the total was 175. This has to be set against a normal battalion strength of 36 officers and just under 1,000 men.[3]

Heavy losses were not a new experience. The 8th Lincolns, a Volunteer Service Battalion formed as part of Kitchener's New Army in the Autumn of 1914, first arrived in France on the 10th September, 1915, with a strength of 28 officers and 995 men. After two weeks march, they were pitched into the Battle of Loos without any previous trench or combat experience. Within a few short hours, they had lost 22 officers and 471 men, including their commanding officer.

Early in the New Year of 1917, Theodore Hardy was to get his first experience of life in the front line. His battalion entered the trenches at Neuve Chapelle, only a few miles north of where they had suffered such terrible losses at Loos, and itself the scene of a disastrous British offensive in March, 1915.

The line ran near the waterlogged meadows of the Lys Valley — now hard frozen and bleak as the east wind blew across the flat landscape. To the south lay the slag heaps and pit heads of the coal field around Loos.

After two years of war, the conflict had come near to stalemate with both sides entrenched in a 'ditch across Europe' stretching from the Channel ports to the Swiss border. A trench newspaper, *The Wipers Times,* described the scene:

'Take a wilderness of ruin, spread with mud quite six feet deep,
In this mud now cut some channels, then you have the line we keep.
Get a lot of Huns and plant them, in a ditch across the way;
Now you have war in the making, as waged from day to day.'[4]

To Editor
The Daily Telegraph.   No.M
135 Fleet Street.   16/3

London E.C.4 — Fearless Padre.

Dear Sir
    Re Tuesday's information Re
Rev. T. B. Hardy brings bright poignant
but fond memories —

    Adjutant to the 8th Lincolnshire
Regiment — I welcomed Mr Hardy
with instructions from the Colonel
that the Padre would please
wait until the return of the Battalion
from the front. Olive Trembles
Mr Hardy demand and was
determined to join the men

in the front line, for he commanded
others. Surely their stayed
at the Base. Mr Hardy was given
I track equipment and a guide
and joined the forward lines
of men. I have never met a man
so unselfish and fearless as
Mr Hardy.

    I may interest your readers
to know that a plaque has been
erected to Mr Hardy — recording his
remarkable achievements — in
Carlisle Cathedral. and also in
Rt Regt School for Boys Nuthurst
where he served as master before
entering the Church.

        Yours faithfully
        F. Brown

*A letter from Captain F. Brown, Adjutant of the 8th Lincolns, recalling
Theodore Hardy's arrival at the front.
The letter was written fifty years on after publicity in the Daily Telegraph about
Hardy's medals being presented to the Chaplains' Department at Bagshot.*

Recruits to the Lincolnshire Regiment at rifle drill in September 1914. The 8th Lincolns were initially all volunteers to Kitchener's 'New Army' and were formed in September 1914. At first there were no uniforms and very few rifles.

'At Lincoln, so many men volunteered that they were lined up in fours on the parade ground and a sergeant walked down the ranks and counted out 1,000 men. When he had enough, he stopped, put his hand out and said:

Winter in the Trenches near Arras, 1917.

When Theodore Hardy first arrived at the front, temperatures were as low as 25 degrees of frost, and the sea froze at Boulogne.

Bernard Martin described his first impressions of the trenches and the advice he was given on his first day thus:

'The front trench, where we lived ... was irregular in depth and width. It had suffered many direct hits by enemy shells and was more or less always under repair. Somehow I had assumed continuous gunfire at the Front, shells falling on the trenches all day, and of course a regular rattle of rifle and machine gun fire. It was almost disquieting to be told there were long periods when war was silent. But the front trench usually had a daily concentrated strafe lasting perhaps thirty minutes and some intermittent shelling at Dawn-Stand-To and Dusk-Stand-To when all troops were on duty, an hour each period. A communication trench connected the front trench with Battalion H.Q., a small group of dug-outs four or five hundred yards back, where Colonel, Second-in-Command and Adjutant lived. All supplies, rations and relieving troops used this communication trench under cover of darkness.

I was told... "Seems a natural impulse to take a quick look over the trench parapet in daylight ... but an impulse to resist. In most parts of the line it would be risky, hereabouts fatal. Very active snipers over the way".'[5]

Robert Graves, answering the question 'What was it like?' wrote:

'Our homes, our privies, our graveyards; like air-raid shelters dug in a muddy field, fenced by a tangle of rusty wire, surrounded by enormous craters, subjected not only to an incessant air-raid of varying intensity, but to constant surprise attacks by professional killers, and without any protection against flooding in times of rain.

And the smells: of corpses, latrine buckets, rotting sandbags, human sweat, chloride of lime, frying bacon. And the sounds; clatter of working parties, rattle of dixie-lids, squeak of rats; laughter and curses and, at sunrise and sunset the cry of "Stand-to".'[6]

Private Jimmy Watson of the 8th Lincolns remembers the cold, the impossibility of getting anything dry and the lice. He also remembers Theodore Hardy:

'He was always with us. He was always in the front line.'[7]

At first neither the officers nor the men took very much notice of Hardy, though when he visited them in the trenches during the day they were always kind to him. Hardy wondered whether if he were to sleep in the day time and visit the trenches at night he might not be more sympathetically received. Accordingly, after his evening meal he made his way to the front line with a knapsack filled with sweets and cigarettes and was 'heartily welcomed and got to know the men well.'[8] By this time, the 'partner' battalion, the 8th Somersets, had been added to his care.

Another memory of Hardy's first few days at the front came from Major-General Bruce-Williams, Commander of the 63rd Infantry Brigade:

'My first introduction to him was at Lestrem in January 1917, when I attended the Battalion Church parade in a field near the village. Mr. Hardy took the service, and I still firmly believe he was asleep standing when saying some of the psalms and prayers. He had most probably been up all night in the trenches! He thought nothing of spending the night in the trenches and waking up in the morning in time to take early Communion and several subsequent parade services.'[9]

Fatigue may explain an incident at this time recalled by a young lieutenant (C. R. Madden) who was himself to win the Military Cross:

'I can well remember an incident which occurred on a Sunday when we were out of the line and billeted in a village. The Padre and myself were quartered in the same room, and I found him sitting on his bed in great distress and even tears.
I discovered the cause to be that his voluntary service had only been attended by some twenty men.
"What do I do that is wrong?" he said. "What is my mistake?"
This was typical of his attitude, and an index to his devotion to duty.'[10]

The truth is probably that the men were too weary to do any other but sleep, and that Hardy's own weariness led to undue introspection and depression. The mood was soon to pass; if the men wouldn't or couldn't come to him, he would go to them, and not necessarily with words but with actions. He told his Divisional Chaplain, G. R. Vallings, that he had decided to live always and entirely with the officers and men in the line whatever the discomforts and dangers, and concluded,

'It is the life which tells; without that preaching is of no use'.

Within days of the conversation, Vallings was to witness the first of an innumerable series of 'Hardy incidents', the rescue of a wounded man in the shadow of the notorious Double Crassier near Lens.

The Double Crassier was two parallel slagheaps of coal waste running at right angles from the German line to the British line across No-Man's-Land. It began at ground level in the German line and rose in height to sixty feet, ending immediately in front of the British line — and allowing the Germans to see directly into the British trenches from an observation post. The British countered this with a one hundred step trench up to a short cross trench within yards of the German observation post. Both sides could hear each other talking, and exceptional precautions had to be taken in a most exposed and dangerous position. It was here that Hardy's first recorded act of heroism took place:

'Two officers, on their way up the trenches, heard groanings and cries for aid, and at last discovered a man lying in the open beyond the parados. He had trusted to the fog, and had been sniped. He was got into some sort of shelter and bandaged, but it was impossible to do more as they were in full view from the notorious Double Crassier; and as the trench was almost up to the knees in mud, there was no use in attempting to move anyone along it.

34

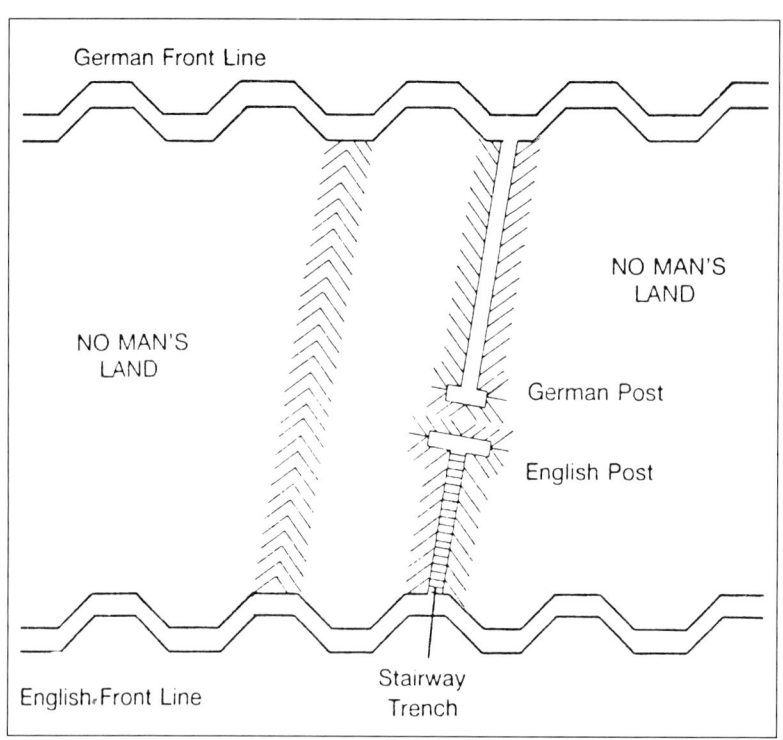

The Double Crassier (Slagheap) near Lens.

Word was taken to the nearest medical aid post, and it was arranged for stretcher bearers to carry him down over the open after darkness had fallen. The man belonged to the Somersets, who had just been relieved that day, and with whom Hardy had come out. When the latter heard of the circumstances nothing would satisfy him but to go up at once, though he sorely needed rest, and though the state of the trenches made walking a very severe strain, and further, he was assured everything possible had been done. I called him an obstinate old man, but I loved him for it. In the salient on more than one occasion he did the same sort of thing when he was absolutely worn out, and only his heroic spirit enabled him to carry on.'[11]

The battalion ended a two month spell of trench duty in mid-March, and began training for the expected Spring offensive. For Theodore Hardy it was a chance to obtain his favourite mode of transport — a bicycle — and delight of delights the opportunity to see his daughter Elizabeth who had recently arrived in France as a V.A.D. Red Cross Nurse. She was based at the Queen Alexandra Hospital in Dunkirk. It was the second day of Spring.

The joy they took in each other's company is evident from the letter they wrote together to William in Egypt. Elizabeth began:

'Dear Will,

This is being written in a tea shop (of course) in a dear little old town a few miles away from my work. I am having the day off and spending it with — guess who — the padre of the 8th Lincolns & Somersets. We only wish you were here. Otherwise the expedition is very like the one we went to Hawkshead nearly a year ago. Father turned up suddenly this morning & I was given the day off. He looks very well — the meat n'est-ce pas?'

'I am still degenerate and rather like it, to tell the truth.'
Elizabeth and her father write to William in March, 1917.

Having had his vegetarian leg pulled, her father takes over the letter . . .

> 'Not a bit of it, though I am still degenerate & rather like it, to tell the truth. I had a good bicycle ride to get here, more than 90 kilos & most of the time against a strong head wind. Got to the Alexandra about 12.30 at night. I am having a splendid day today: We are going back now (walking) to ———— and there to dinner at a rather swell place, with bathrooms and water — Best love from both.'[12]

One can only speculate at the thoughts of this 53 year old little cleric as he cycled the 60 miles across northern France to see his much loved daughter. But of one thing there can be little doubt, it must have seemed like Heaven on Earth to have had a hot bath and dinner in a 'swell place' after two months of ice, mud, bullets and death in the trenches.

[1] Colonel Repington, *The First World War, 1914-18*, Constable, 1920.

[2] Haig Diary, 9th February, 1917.

[3] Casualty Figures obtained from, Simpson, *The History of the Lincolnshire Regiment, 1914-18*, Medici Society, 1931.

Middlebrook, himself a Lincolnshire man, quotes the difficulties facing a stretcher bearer in the 8th Lincolns (Sgt. A. P. Britton) on the first day of the Somme:

'As we had no stretchers we had to use sheets of corrugated iron and by the end of the day we had all cut our fingers.'

Martin Middlebrook, *The First Day of the Somme*, p.228, Allen Lane, 1971.

[4] *The Wipers Times*, a trench newspaper.

[5] Martin, *op. cit.* pp.47/48.

[6] *The Sunday Times*, 9th November, 1958.

[7] Interview with author, 10th August, 1986.

[8] Mary Hardy, *op. cit.*

[9] *Ibid.*

[10] *Ibid.* Captain Madden was to receive a bar to his M.C. during the German attack in which Theodore Hardy received his fatal wound. By this time he was a Company Commander in the 8th Somersets.

[11] *Ibid.*

[12] Letter dated 22nd March (1917) in possession of Miss Patricia Hardy (William's daughter). William was serving as a doctor in a Military Hospital at Alexandria.

OVER THE TOP: ARRAS, APRIL 1917

'"Good morning, Good morning!" the General said,
When we met him last week on our way to the line.
Now the soldiers he smiled at are most of 'em dead,
And we're cursing his staff for incompetent swine.

"He's a cheery old card" grunted Harry to Jack
As they slogged up to Arras with rifle and pack . . .
But he did for them both by his plan of attack.'
The General, Siegfried Sassoon.

Weary stalemate continued throughout the Western Front during the first four months of Theodore Hardy's service there. But elsewhere profound and significant changes had taken place.

Only seven days before the Padre of the 8th Lincolns and his daughter enjoyed tea together, the Tsar of all the Russias was deposed and it was to be only a matter of months before Russia left the war completely.

Two weeks after the Hardys met, America entered the war, provoked by unrestricted U-boat warfare and an astonishing German effort to incite Mexico to attack the U.S.A.

In Britain, the mercurial and devious Lloyd George had replaced the exhausted Asquith as Prime Minister. The French Government meanwhile had replaced their Commander-in-Chief, the ponderous taciturn 'Papa' Joffre, with the aggressive and over self-confident Nivelle.

Nivelle's boast, 'We have the formula', combined with his fluent English, made an immediate appeal to Lloyd George. Relations between the British Prime Minister and his own Commander-in-Chief Haig, were marked by mutual suspicion, mistrust and intrigue.

Lloyd George backed Nivelle's new plan for a massive French attack on a thirty mile front in the Champagne area, not only to take pressure off the British troops, but also to undermine Haig's authority. This was to be 'the decisive blow' which would win the war, according to Nivelle. On the 9th April a British attack to the north in the Arras area would act as a diversion. The French attack would commence on 16th April.

The Germans were fully aware of the French plans. They were also making preparations to fight a defensive war until such time as the U-boat campaign succeeded and forces could be redeployed from the Russian front. A massive defence system (known as the 'Siegfried line' in Germany and the 'Hindenburg line' to the allies) was constructed from near Arras south to the Aisne. Throughout March the Germans quietly withdrew to this line. They destroyed and booby trapped an area twenty miles deep and sixty miles long between the existing front and the new defence line. They then waited for the Allies to attack.

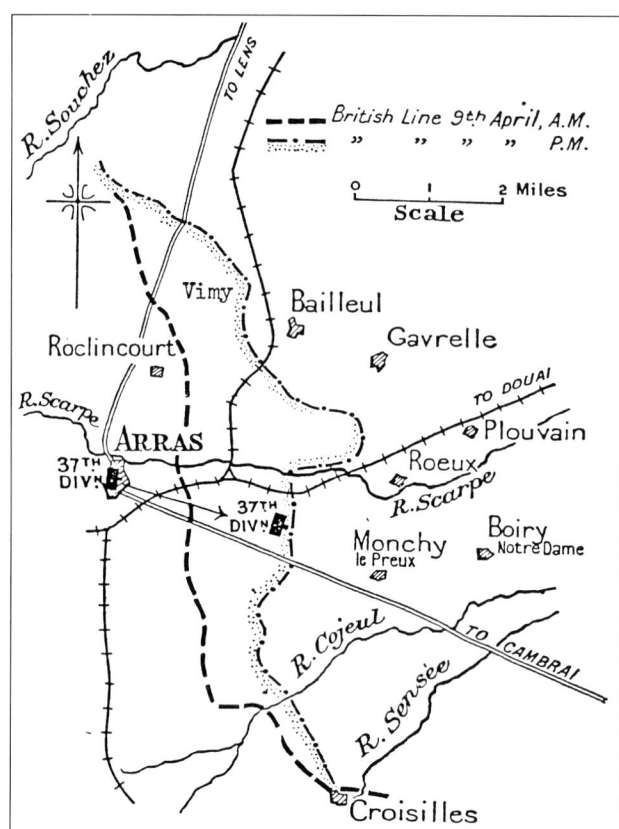

THE BATTLE OF ARRAS, 9th APRIL, 1917

The 8th Lincolns and 8th Somersets were part of the 37th Division.

Six other Divisions attacked to the south, whilst ten Divisions including the Canadians, attacked to the north towards Vimy Ridge.

In the north, the objective was to capture the heavily defended and strategically important Vimy Ridge.

In the south, the intention was to turn the northern flank of the Hindenburg line and drive on to Cambrai.

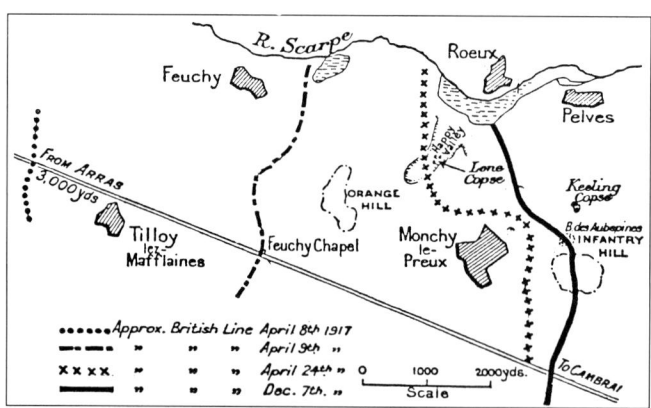

63rd Infantry Brigade (8th Lincolns, 8th Somersets, 10th Yorks & Lancs., 4th Middlesex) attacked along the northern edge of the Arras-Cambrai road.

The immediate objective was Orange Hill. Theodore Hardy accompanied the attack, helping to set up the Advanced Dressing Station at Feuchy Chapel.

On Easter Monday, 9th April, the 8th Lincolns and 8th Somersets, their Padre with them, went 'over the top.' They knew nothing of the background intrigues or overall strategy. Their function was to do their duty and to capture Orange Hill.

The Lincolns assembled for the attack by way of sewers and tunnels through the ancient but by now battered town of Arras so as not to be seen by the enemy. Each man carried half his own weight in equipment: rifle, bayonet, steel helmet, entrenching tool, full waterbottle, groundsheet, two days' rations, three sandbags, 170 rounds of rifle ammunition, two Mills bombs, and a flare to assist reconnaissance aircraft. In view of this weight it was decided not to wear greatcoats. As soon as this decision was made the snow and sleet began to fall!

Three lines of German trenches lay between Arras and Feuchy Chapel, and all were captured by troops of 12th Division during the 9th April. 37th Division passed through during the day as a second wave, and by midnight the Lincolns and Somersets had captured Orange Hill. For the next three days they were to face fierce resistance as they gradually advanced and helped to capture Monchy-le-Preux. There were heavy casualties, including the commanding officer of the Lincolns.

Siegfried Sassoon, who was wounded in the Arras offensive, writes of 'an emotional padre who was painfully aware that he could do nothing except stand about and feel sympathetic.'[1] If Sassoon had been taken to Feuchy Chapel Dressing Station, literary history may have taken a different turn.

Hardy at once got to work carrying the wounded on stretchers from the front. His ambulance class training at Kirkby Lonsdale was put to good effect. He made notes so as to write to the relatives of the dead and wounded. The men knew him and trusted him, his quiet courage gave them strength and calm, and when they asked for it he would quietly pray with them. His colleague Geoffrey Vallings, D.S.O., has a different story to Siegfried Sassoon:

> 'During the first Arras battle, April 9th, I directed him to proceed with one of the medical officers who was to form an advanced dressing station within the German lines if the attack proved successful. Being with the A.D.M.S. when the location was chosen, I pushed on to select a further site and bearer posts. Late at night I returned to the position about one kilometre beyond Tilloy on the Arras-Cambrai road, and found Hardy had been continuously at work for about thirty-six hours, so I ordered him to bed. You must remember that always he would obey me, not merely because I was his senior in rank, but because we were practically the same age. He wrapped himself in a blanket and slept like a child in the corner of a ruined cellar. There is extant a photograph of the dressing station, in which Hardy is distinctly recognisable, but I was never able to procure one. It appeared, unless my memory betrays me, in either the *Daily Mirror* or *Sketch*.'[2]

The Imperial War Museum very kindly searched their photographic collection and have found the photograph Mr. Vallings was unable to obtain. Theodore Hardy gazes

Advance Dressing Station, Feuchy Chapel. Theodore Hardy can be seen peering over the shoulder of a German prisoner and a British Corporal at a wounded man on a

with intent concern at a wounded soldier carried by a British corporal and three German prisoners. In the foreground the dead await burial. Easter Monday was never like this in Hutton Roof, although Hardy must have pondered the similarity with a hill at Golgotha.

At first, the battle gave the illusion of success. The Canadians spectacularly stormed Vimy Ridge, and the 37th Division achieved a penetration of five miles. Allenby, commanding the 3rd Army, believed the breakthrough had come and issued the order that he . . . 'wishes all troops to understand that the 3rd Army is now pursuing a defeated enemy and that risks must be freely taken.'[3]

It didn't seem like that at the front, although Allenby, believing in the breakthrough, sent in the cavalry. A Gordon Highlander watched them near Monchy-le-Preux:

> 'During a lull in the snowstorm an excited shout was raised that our cavalry were coming up! Sure enough, away behind us, moving quickly in extended order down the slope of Orange Hill, was line upon line of mounted men as far as we could see . . . It may have been a fine sight, but it was a wicked waste of men and horses, for the enemy immediately opened on them a hurricane of every kind of missile. If the cavalry advanced through us at a trot or canter, they came back at a gallop, including dismounted men and riderless horses . . .
>
> They left numbers of dead and wounded among us, but the horses seem to have suffered most, and for a while after we put bullets into poor brutes that were aimlessly limping about on three legs, or careering madly in their agony like one I saw with the whole of its muzzle blown away.'[4]

Such was Theodore Hardy's introduction to the Arras offensive. On the night of 12th April his battalion was pulled out and relieved. By the 14th April, Allenby's determination to keep attacking, despite horrific losses and dreadful conditions of swirling snow in which units lost touch with each other, had brought a written protest from three of his Divisional generals. Haig called a halt — until the weather improved nine days later and the offensive started again.

Geoffrey Vallings again remembered Hardy's involvement and attitude:

> 'During the second Arras battle we attacked Greenland Hill, north of the Scarpe, between Gavrelle and the Roeux chemical works. On this occasion I insisted upon Hardy going back to the main dressing station at Haut Avesnes (five miles west of Arras), and I do not think he ever forgave me. I am satisfied that this probably saved his life.
>
> Our casualties were very severe, our positions exposed, and several Commanding Officers were killed. Hardy would certainly have run risks in ministering to the wounded. One Chaplain was killed, another severely wounded, more than one besides had had very narrow escapes.
>
> Whenever possible I relieved Hardy myself, and had simply to force him into bed, but so tired was he that he fell asleep directly his head touched the pillow. His ministrations were simply invaluable and his devotion absolutely untiring.

Advanced Dressing Station, Feuchy Chapel near Tilloy, 10th April 1917. Hardy is clearly recognisable in the centre background, whilst bodies await burial in the

On several occasions during our few days' rest before taking over the Wancourt-Guemappe line Hardy had several talks with me. He remonstrated over my sending him back, and pleaded to go forward in the next battle then impending. This gave me the deepest insight into his character. I argued with him that he owed a duty to myself, as his senior, and to his brother Chaplains; that if he were knocked out it would involve more work for us; that an older man with more experience was specially useful with a crowd of wounded and dying men, and that a live Hardy was much more valuable to everyone than a dead hero. He told me that he was a dreadful coward, but he felt sure that the forward area was the place for him, supplementing his plea with a great deal that I cannot repeat, and that I should spoil in the attempt. Here let me bear witness to the fact that Hardy's courage was no inability to appreciate danger nor any sort of blind physical pluck, which nerves but few. Its source was complete confidence in his Master.

He was never regardless or unconscious of danger, but his spirit rose supreme above it. He looked upon his wife as alive with him, in constant communion and fellowship. He loved his children intensely, but he believed that he could do no better, if God so willed, than join his beloved wife in the presence of their Lord. Death, as many of us regard it, simply did not exist for him.

I cannot reproduce it all except with more time than is at my disposal; indeed, probably I could not do so at all — it is beyond me altogether. But the faith and love were so intensely beautiful that at the close of one particular conversation, when his Brigade was already on the line of march, and we were talking with our horses' reins on our arms, I was unable to speak. I was in the presence of a saint, and the Master Himself was standing by. I never argued again.'[5]

The Lincolns suffered terribly in the Arras offensive with a total of 524 casualties — over half the Battalion's strength. The battle left 30,000 of Haig's soldiers dead and 128,000 wounded. Twelve months later, the ground gained over a month's hard fighting was lost in a few short hours.

In the south, Nivelle's French offensive was a disastrous failure. Within days it ground to a halt with over 200,000 casualties. Mutiny erupted throughout the French Army and Nivelle was dismissed. Somehow, Petain restored order, but the French were clearly in no condition to continue any sort of offensive action and it was unlikely that they could resist any major German attack. The initiative now rested with Haig. He was to make his move in Flanders, towards a place called Passchendaele.

---

[1] Sassoon, *op. cit.*

[2] Letter from Reverend Geoffrey Vallings, D.S.O. (Senior Chaplain to 37th Division), to Mrs Mary Hardy, 1919.

[3] General Edmund Allenby, Order of the Day issued 12th April, 1917 to 3rd Army units.

[4] Eyewitness account. Private in 1st Gordon Highlanders, quoted in Lloyd, *opus cit.* p.151.

[5] Vallings, *ibid.*

Commanding Officers of the 8th Battalion The Somerset Light Infantry

LT.-COL. J. W. SCOTT, D.S.O.
Commanded 8th Battalion

LT.-COL. C. J. DE B. SHERINGHAM, D.S.O., M.C.
Commanded 8th Battalion

Colonel Scott was killed leading the Battalion into action at Greenland Hill, Arras on 23rd April, 1917.

Geoffrey Vallings was to write: 'On this occasion I insisted upon Hardy going back to the main dressing station at Haut-Avesnes, and I do not think he ever forgave me. I am satisfied that this probably saved his life.'

Colonel Sheringham took over command after the death of Colonel Hardyman on 24th August, 1918.

He was to say of Hardy, 'I shall often think of a figure, with a waterproof sheet folded over his arms, standing at a little distance away in a shy, unobtrusive and almost apologetic manner. I shall never forget the expression of the men when the news came that the Padre was dead.'

Horse Ambulances wait to take away the wounded from the Advanced Dressing Station near Tilloy, 10th April, 1917. Hardy can be seen standing in front of the canvas shelter attached to the building.

'STUCK FAST IN THE MUD'
By Alexander Jamieson

Jamieson was a Captain in the 10th York and Lancaster Regiment, one of the four Battalions (along with the 8th Lincolns, 8th Somersets and 4th Middlesex) in the 63rd Infantry Brigade.

The incident occurred at Oostaverne: the same circumstances and place in which Theodore Hardy was awarded the D.S.O. In this case there was a happier ending, the man survived. Jamieson wrote:

> 'The beginning of an awful experience! One of the 10th Service Battalion York and Lancaster Regiment got held fast by the mud and slime in a shell hole which flooded as he struggled.
> To haul him with ropes was impossible as he would have died.
> It took four nights' hard work by the Pioneers to get him free.
> His comrade stood by him day and night under fire. He fed him by means of a long stick. When eventually saved both went delirious.'

WAITING FOR A MAN TO DIE
OOSTAVERNE, FLANDERS, FRIDAY 3rd AUGUST, 1917

'Wherefore Christian was left to tumble in the Slough of Despond alone ... but could not get out because of the burden that was upon his back: but I beheld in my dream, that a man came to him, whose name was Help.'
Pilgrim's Progress, John Bunyan

The mud stank in his nostrils and his whole body shivered with wet and cold. The pain in his wrist kept him awake although he was at the very edge of his endurance.

He was waiting for a man to die. It couldn't be long now. He knew now what it must have been like at the foot of that Cross at Golgotha. 'Lord, now lettest Thy Servant depart in peace.'

The rain had gone on and on it seemed for ever. Odd how the poppies cling to life when everything else has surrendered. The roses must be out now in the garden at Hutton Roof. I wonder what Elizabeth is doing? I wonder if Will is coping with the heat in Alexandria? Is there still a world out there?

The man moved and groaned. He was up to his neck in the slime. 'It's all right. I'm still here. I'll stay with you.'

He'd sat with Florence like this, but when he came back from the Church she had gone. Waiting, waiting. Is it Thursday or Friday? It doesn't matter, I suppose. What is time anyway? It's a puzzle how it goes so slowly and so quickly. 'It's all right, I'm still here.'

Do you remember the smell of the juniper on the Cragg? We used to look at the stars and realise how small we are. I hope Wilson is safe ...

'The Son of man must suffer many things, and be rejected of the elders and chief priests and scribes, and be raised the third day' — 'It's all right. I'm still here. I'll stay with you.'

I never knew it could be so cold in August. Do you remember the wind in your face coming down Lupton Hill on the bike? We used to walk on the Cragg in the rain, but it wasn't as cold as this.

'Come on, Padre. He's gone. You can't do any more. For goodness sake you're cold. Let me rub your legs . . . Put this blanket round his shoulders . . . Now come on, and keep your head down.'

'No, I must read the burial service. You can join in if you wish.'

'I am the resurrection and the life . . . '

* * * * *

Much later they gave him a D.S.O. — some people said it should have been a V.C.

'Somehow, it didn't seem to matter and it was all rather embarrassing really. It wasn't much, was it? If anybody should have had a medal it was that young lad in the mud. He's dead and I'm still alive.'

A PLACE CALLED PASSCHENDAELE

'I died in Hell . . . They called it Passchendaele'

Memorial Tablet, Siegfried Sassoon

The third Battle of Ypres, better known as the Passchendaele Offensive, lasted from 31st July to 10th November, 1917. The British gained seven miles of Flemish slime and mud at the cost of at least 265,000 casualties. The defending Germans (who had lost 200,000) recaptured it all six months later.

What was to become known as the 'battle of the mud', was planned as a clean breakthrough to the Flanders coast. It turned into a battle of attrition where men drowned in shell holes filled with rain, and where horses and mules literally disappeared into craters of slime. In this hellish place Theodore Hardy was awarded the Distinguished Service Order and the Military Cross.

After their heavy losses at Arras, the 8th Lincolns spent most of May and June in billets integrating a new influx of conscripts. Towards the end of June they marched sixty miles north to the Ypres sector, taking over trenches near Wytschaete.

Wytschaete lay astride the Messines Ridge captured from the Germans just three weeks before the arrival of the Lincolns. The capture of Messines Ridge had been one of the few spectacular successes in an otherwise stalemate situation. Eight miles of German trench-line had been mined from underground tunnels constructed over the previous two years. On 7th June nineteen enormous explosions destroyed the trench system; the total charge of just under one million pounds of high explosive was heard in London. British troops captured and held on to the ridge. Hardy's mentor Geoffrey Studdert-Kennedy was awarded the Military Cross in the subsequent German counter-attacks.

The seven week delay between the capture of Messines Ridge and the opening of the main offensive towards Passchendaele was to be of critical importance in allowing the Germans to consolidate their defensive positions. Paradoxically, the delay was the result of Lloyd George's lack of faith in Haig's ability to undertake an offensive without heavy losses on the scale of the Somme. Lloyd George eventually agreed to the Passchendaele offensive with the pre-condition that it be discontinued if casualties were incommensurate with the ground gained. Having got his way, Haig went on to ignore this condition, optimistically convinced in his own mind that,

> 'Germany is within 4 to 6 months of a date at which she will be unable to maintain the strength of her units in the field . . . Germany may well be forced to conclude peace on our terms before the end of the year.'[1]

For two weeks before the infantry attack due on 31st July, the Lincolns and Somersets in their trenches east of Wytschaete witnessed the heaviest British artillery bombardment yet on the German positions. Shells ceaselessly screamed overhead day and night from behind them, whilst German artillery fired back at them wounding the 8th Somersets C.O. and several of the men.

King George V, followed by General Plumer and the Prince of Wales, tour the Messines Ridge near Wytschaete after one million pounds of high explosive placed in nineteen underground tunnels destroyed the German trench system. The sound of the explosion could be heard in London.

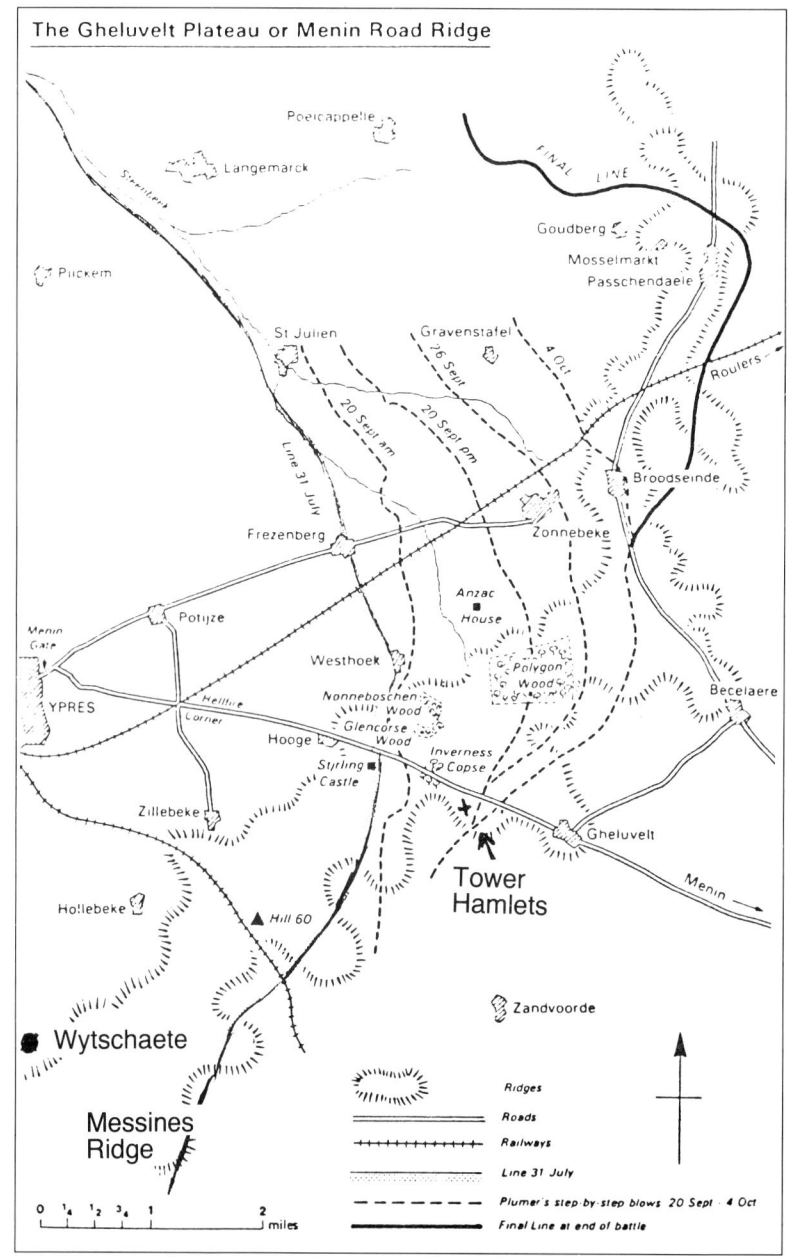

The Gheluvelt Plateau or Menin Road Ridge

The Passchendaele Offensive, 1917

Hardy won his D.S.O. to the East of Wytschaete at Oostaverne, and his M.C. near Hill 60.

Private Sage of the 8th Somersets won his V.C. at Tower Hamlets on 4th October.

The British bombardment was intended to destroy enemy positions, thus easing the task of the infantry when they went over the top. Yet it had the effect of turning the ground over which they were to attack into a muddy nightmare. It totally smashed the delicate system of pipes and dykes draining the low lying Flanders fields, and as the bombardment ceased the rain came down.

At 3.00 a.m. on 31st July, Private Jimmy Watson of the 8th Lincolns remembers being given the tablespoon of rum by his Platoon Officer that always preceded going over the top,

'We always knew that was it when we were given the rum.'[2]

At 3.50 a.m. the whistle blew and they climbed out of the trenches, Theodore Hardy their Padre going with them. 'He always came with us', said Private Watson.

The fighting was confused, although by the end of the day:

'The line gained by 63rd Brigade on 31st July varied in depth from a few yards to 400 yards.'[3]
'Some stiff close-quarter fighting ensued, and heavy casualties were inflicted on the enemy, but the attackers were hard pressed.'[4]
'D Company of the Lincolns and a Company of the 4th Middlesex fought it out where they were until they were all either killed or wounded.'[5]

The Adjutant of the 8th Somersets described Theodore Hardy's response to the situation that night:

'About 11 p.m. . . . the Germans were shelling our position very heavily; about fifty or sixty had been killed and wounded at one spot. The night was pitch dark, the shelling about the worst I have ever known, and the crying of the wounded and dying such that I shall never forget. The heavy shelling went on all the night and until about 3 a.m. next morning. Amid those terrible scenes that "Saint of God" remained the whole time, helping to bandage the wounds and to carry the wounded to a dressing station some 300 to 400 yards away, which was also being badly shelled. The next morning the shelling had abated, and, looking round to see what damage had been done, I saw a man on the ground some little way off. It was the Dear Old Padre.
At first we thought he was dead, but no. He had worked all night until he was absolutely exhausted, and dropped down where he had been working. We woke him, wishing to take him back where he could have food and rest, but he insisted upon first burying those who had fallen during the night, and nothing would persuade him to leave until this was accomplished.'[6]

On the night of 1st/2nd August the exhausted Lincolns and Somersets were relieved by the 13th Rifle Brigade. The Lincolns had suffered 177 casualties and the Somersets 155. They were to have two weeks' rest before re-joining the line. Yet after only one night's rest, the 13th Rifle Brigade discovered that one man had returned — a small elderly padre.

Within a few hours they were to be grateful to him. A Staff Captain remembered his arrival and gives us a vivid description of Hardy:

'I was interviewing a driver, who had reported for orders as to whether to unload some ammunition, or to take it further forward, when a Padre approached me.

I shall often think of a figure, with a waterproof sheet folded over his arms, standing at a little distance away in a shy, unobtrusive and almost apologetic manner.

I may say in passing that one of Padre Hardy's particular characteristics, as I learnt later, was that he found it extremely difficult to find his way about, which added very greatly to the distance covered by him, and consequently to the fatigue and difficulty of any task.

"Would you be good enough," he said, "to tell me how to get up to the line?"

I asked him if he had ever been up there before and gathered that he had, but he didn't seem to know where he was, and I hated to let him go without a guide, so suggested, as it was getting late, that he should stay, and have something to eat, and that we could give him shelter for the night in what was called the Dormitory, a large shelter with six bunks.

This the Padre accepted: he said he should be up very early in the morning, and would make arrangements to go up to the line with one of the runners.

I handed him over to one of the officers who was looking after the Divisional Ammunition Dump, and saw no more of him.

This was most characteristic; he said not a word of his mission, but just quietly went to work. Next morning he went to the forward post, out into "No Man's Land", and remained there between thirty six and forty eight hours by the side of a soldier who had been bogged, and was three parts submerged in the mud. He fed him to keep him alive, and worked with others the whole of the following night trying to extricate him.'[7]

The reason for Theodore Hardy's return was that he could not forget what he had seen during the attack by the Lincolns and Somersets. He knew that wounded men still lay trapped in the mud in 'No Man's Land' and he could not abandon them:

'In the attack on July 31st, the (63rd) Brigade attacked on the Wambeke Stream (East of Wytschaete) and the ground was in such a sodden condition that many men were buried up to their shoulders, and being under the close and accurate fire of the enemy, it was only possible to try and extricate them by night. For several nights after the action, Mr. Hardy assisted in extricating these poor fellows and in getting some food to them: on the third morning he was reported missing and could not be found for many hours. He was then found lying exhausted and asleep in a wet shell hole near the front line; so exacting had his labours been for the two previous nights he had collapsed from sheer fatigue.'[8]

Hardy had in fact stayed with a dying man during the day as well as the night, talking to him, encouraging him, feeding him and enduring constant sniper and machine gun fire. He had, himself, suffered a broken wrist, but he would not abandon the man until death intervened. Much to Hardy's own astonishment, he was awarded the D.S.O.

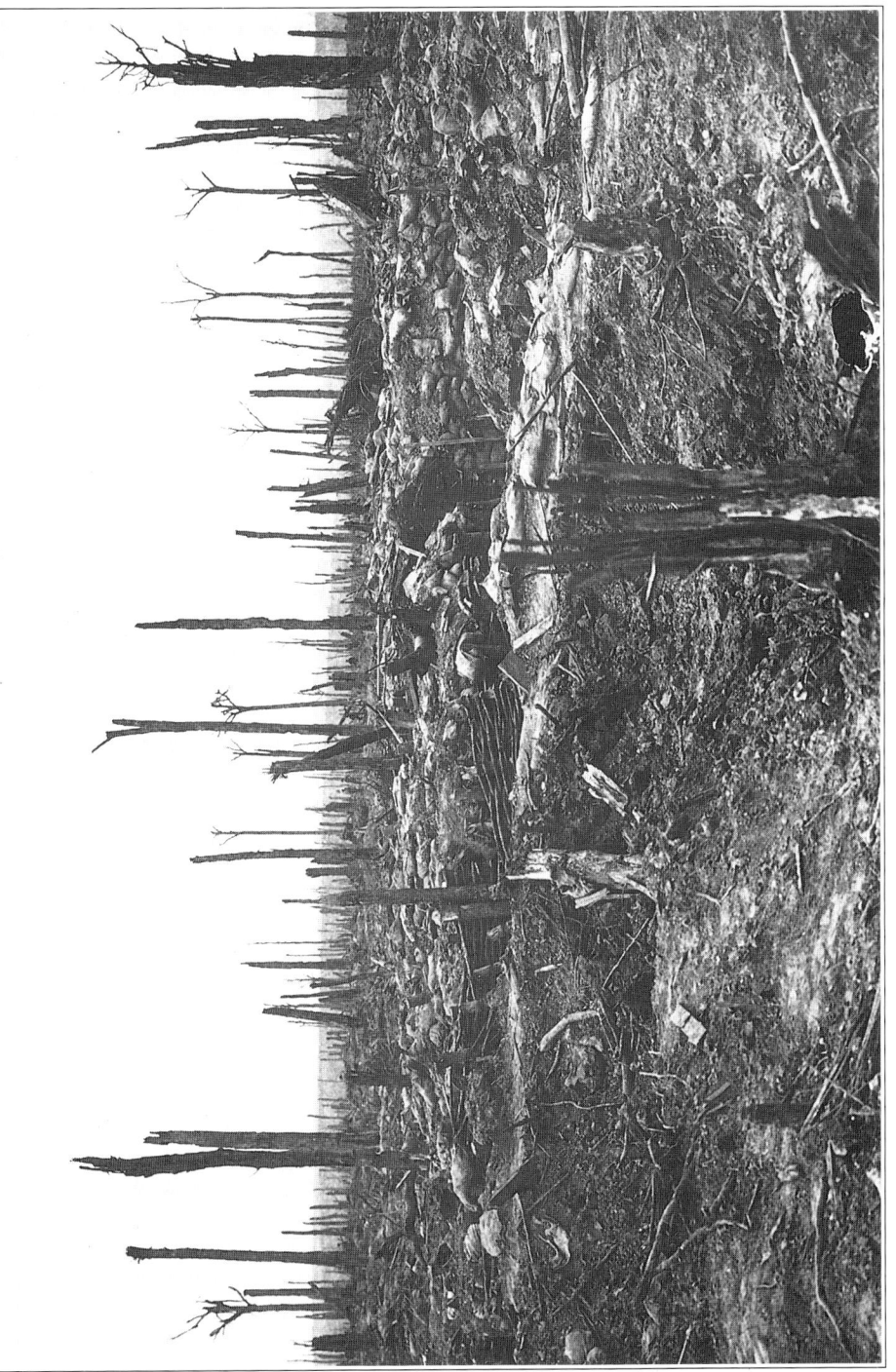

Oostaverne in the Passchendaele offensive. Here Theodore Hardy was awarded the D.S.O. for staying with a dying man trapped in the mud of a shell hole. They were under enemy fire, yet despite Hardy's own broken wrist he stayed with the man for over 36 hours giving what comfort and support he could.

for this episode which was recorded in the citation published in the *London Gazette:*

> '*DISTINGUISHED SERVICE ORDER, REV. THEODORE BAYLEY HARDY,*
> *London Gazette,* published 18th October, 1917
> *London Gazette,* details 7th March, 1918
> Army Chaplains Department, att'd 8th Battalion Lincolnshire Regiment
>
> "For conspicuous gallantry and devotion to duty in volunteering to go with a rescue party for some men who had been left stuck in the mud the previous night between the enemy's outpost line and our own. All the men except one were brought in. He then organised a party for the rescue of this man, and remained with it all night, though under rifle fire at close range, which killed one of the party. With his left arm in splints, owing to a broken wrist, and under the worst weather conditions, he crawled out with patrols to within seventy yards of the enemy and remained with wounded men under heavy fire".[9]

According to Geoffrey Vallings, the award would have been the Victoria Cross if sufficient eye witnesses could have been found. Hence, also, the delay from August.[10]

Despite the horrors described in the Chapter thus far, the major British effort had been concentrated to the north of Hardy's position, above the Ypres to Menin Road. Throughout August, Gough's Fifth Army had led the offensive to the north east of Ypres. By the 16th August, Gough had had enough,

> 'The state of the ground was by this time frightful. The labour of bringing up supplies and ammunition, of moving or firing guns, which had often sunk up to their axles, was a fearful strain on the officers and men . . . When it came to the advance of the infantry for an attack, across water-logged shell holes, movement was so slow and fatiguing that only the shortest advances could be contemplated. In consequence I informed the Commander-in-Chief that tactical success was not possible . . . and advised that the attack should now be abandoned.'[11]
>
> But Haig would not accept this. He, 'thought that he was killing a lot of Germans.'[12]

By the end of August, though, Haig decided to switch tactics, transferring the offensive from Gough to Plumer's Second Army further south. Now it would be the turn of Hardy's comrades to take the full impact of the offensive.

There was a three week pause throughout September as Plumer made his preparations. He decided upon a limited number of short advances preceded by systematic and thorough shelling of the enemy positions with a creeping barrage. Attacks took place on the 20th and the 26th September. The Lincolns and Somersets were to take part in the third attack on the 4th October, towards Gheluvelt on the Menin Road. The rain started again.

The mud of Passchendaele. It could take as many as eight men to move a stretcher. "That Hardy is the finest chap I have ever seen; he is not content to go out with one squad of bearers, he goes out with all. By God, he deserves every decoration a man can win!"

R.A.M.C. Corporal.

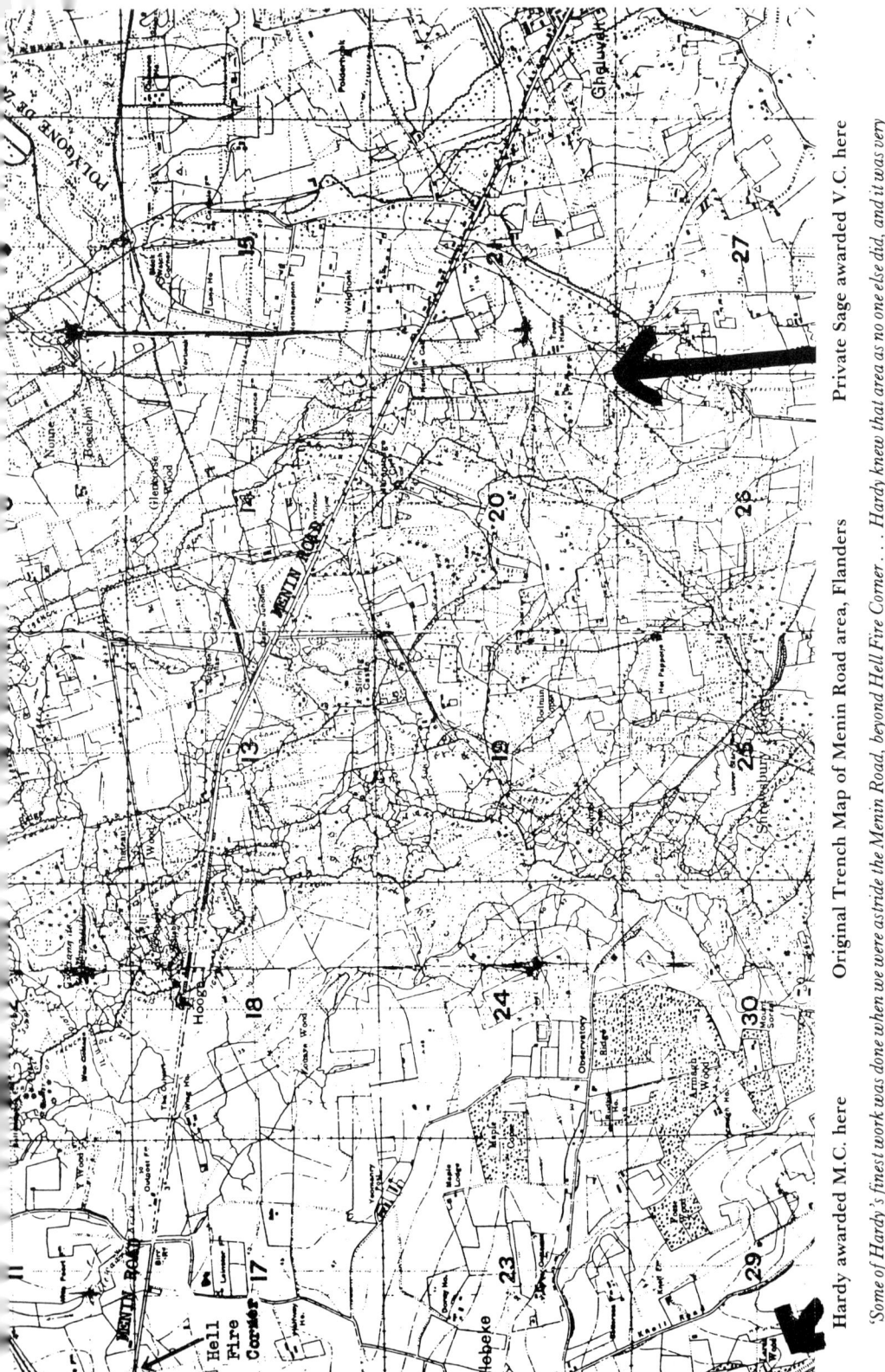

Hardy awarded M.C. here   Original Trench Map of Menin Road area, Flanders   Private Sage awarded V.C. here

'Some of Hardy's finest work was done when we were astride the Menin Road, beyond Hell Fire Corner . . . Hardy knew that area as no one else did, and it was very

Chateau Wood, Flanders in the Autumn of 1917.

It was in the attack of 4th October that Private Thomas Sage of the 8th Somersets was awarded the Victoria Cross. It was the supreme award for an act of supreme unselfishness, care for others and sheer spontaneous courage.

Sage was in a shell hole with eight others at the Tower Hamlets spear east of Ypres. One of the men was shot by the enemy whilst in the act of throwing a bomb. The live bomb fell into the shell hole, and Private Sage immediately threw himself on it in order to save the lives of his comrades. Amazingly, Sage survived but suffered very severe wounds. Hardy helped to care for him at the Advanced Dressing Station.

Geoffrey Vallings was to write of this attack:

> 'Some of Hardy's finest work was done when we were astride the Menin Road, beyond Hell Fire Corner . . . The Boche bombardments were terrific, possibly the worst in my own experience. Hardy knew that area as no one else did, and it was very difficult to relieve him. A Corporal in the R.A.M.C. said in my hearing, though without being aware of my presence, "That Hardy is the finest chap I have ever seen; he is not content to go out with one squad of bearers, he goes out with all. By God, he deserves every decoration a man can win". I may mention that in less than a week we lost over one hundred stretcher-bearers knocked out in one way or another.'[13]

Conditions were so appalling at this time, that it would sometimes take as many as eight men to carry one stretcher. For a man approaching his fifty fourth birthday the physical demands must have been extremely punishing.

Within days Hardy was indeed to win another award; this time the Military Cross. The event took place near the notorious Hill 60 as he was passing an artillery battery on his way, inevitably to the front line. His friend and colleague Geoffrey Vallings was a witness to what happened:

> 'That Hardy was difficult to relieve was his own doing, as it was so impossible to find him. I had arranged to meet him at the Larch Wood tunnels. On my arrival a message was given to me that having had a good sleep he needed no relief, and had gone up the line. He had played this trick before, so I determined to follow and find him. Between the Canada Street and Larch Wood tunnels ran a light railway which we utilised for bringing down wounded on trucks.
>
> Hardy was coming down with two R.A.M.C. men in charge, when a man from a heavy battery not far away shouted that they had some severely injured. At the same moment the Boche opened an appalling bombardment. No other word will describe it, so you must excuse me saying it was absolute hell. However the job was done, though how anyone lived through it is a mystery to myself. The whole surface of the ground seemed to be shot away. On this occasion, as on many another, Hardy's calm confidence was an inspiration. He received most deservedly the Military Cross, and the two other men the Medal. Over and over again his courageous example has nerved me to try and follow his lead, as to my knowledge it has many others.'[14]

Geoffrey Vallings' own modesty stands out in this account. He was himself awarded the D.S.O.

* * * * *

Larch Wood and Canada Tunnels near Hill 60. Men look up from loading ammunition on to the light railway as a shell bursts on the ridge. Hardy was awarded the Military Cross here in October, 1917, for rescuing a group of severely wounded men under heavy artillery fire.

'It was absolute hell. However, the job was done, though how anyone lived through it is a mystery to myself. The whole surface of the ground seemed to be shot away. Hardy's calm confidence was an inspiration.'

Geoffrey Vallings.

The rubble that was Passchendaele village finally fell to the Canadians on 6th November. The following day Haig's Chief of Staff, General Kiggell, paid his first visit to the combat zone. As his car lurched along the Menin Road through the swampland he became more and more agitated. Finally he burst into tears and muttered, 'Good God, did we really send men to fight in that?' His companion, who had been through the campaign, replied, 'It's worse further up.'[15]

* * * * *

The mud turned to ice, but the 8th Lincolns and 8th Somersets continued on trench duty in the Ypres sector throughout the winter.

In due course, Theodore Hardy was presented with his D.S.O. and M.C. much against his wishes, and indeed under protest. Lt. Col. Hitch, Commanding Officer of the 8th Lincolns wrote, 'His retiring nature made it almost a penance to wear those ribbons which most of us would give our right arm for.'[16] The Commander of the 63rd Infantry Brigade noticed that Hardy would 'place his left arm across his breast to hide his decorations when he was speaking to a soldier who himself had no such decoration.'[17]

Whenever his own battalions were relieved, Hardy would stay in the front line with the relieving battalion. He was 'handed over as a trench store.'[18]

Another memory of Theodore Hardy at this time came from the Somersets' Sergeant Major:

'My job was to see that the Companies in the line were supplied with rations, water etc. . . . and for that we used carrying parties . . . it was a difficult job as the ground was in such a condition, and very often men got stuck in the mud: Mr Hardy would come along and ask the time the party was going up, so that he would be able to go up with them.

His main object in going was to help the men with their loads. Many a night has he carried up rations for a fellow who was not so able as the others. All he used to think about was helping others, never about himself. I often used to think he would be overdoing it, and be taken ill, as he was always on the go . . . .

After the rations had been handed over, he would proceed to the outpost line, where he would remain 'til it was too light to remain any longer. It was not very often he missed a post, which were very difficult to find, what with the conditions of the ground and the black nights: and he would always remain in the dangerous places the longest, cheering everybody up as he visited each post.'[19]

Seventy years on, Private Jimmy Watson of the 8th Lincolns still remembers the Padre's nightly visits to the outposts. 'It's only me, boys', he would say. He would bring cigarettes and sweets and sometimes read to us. He would take letters back to post for us.'[20]

Jimmy Watson's Commanding Officer summed up the 8th Lincolns' feelings about their 'Dear Old Padre':

The mud of Passchendaele. Hardy visited men in trenches such as this every night without fail. He would help to carry rations and supplies. For a man of fifty four, the physical stress must have been punishing.

'He was to all of us, who troubled to think a little below the surface, as nearly a true Christian as one can ever expect to meet on earth. He appealed to us all, both officers and men, by his absolute fearlessness, physical and moral, and by his simple sincerity and lack of cant or humbug. We loved him for his self-effacing devotion to duty.'[21]

* * * * *

On 21st March, 1918, news came of a massive German attack to the south in the area of the Somme. The British 3rd and 5th Armies were forced back and were in a desperate situation. The two battalions were rushed south to re-inforce the line. They found themselves in Gommecourt looking across to the shattered stumps of Rossignol Wood.

[1] Haig, Despatch to War Cabinet, 12th June, 1917.
[2] Interview with author, 10th August, 1986.
[3] Wyrall, *History of the Somerset Light Infantry, 1914-1919,* pp.194-197. Methuen, 1927.
[4] *Ibid.*
[5] *Ibid.*
[6] Captain H. O. Pring, M.C., letter to Mary Hardy, 1919, *op. cit.*
[7] Lt. Col C. J. de B. Sheringham D.S.O., M.C., letter to Mary Hardy, 1919. Sheringham was a Staff Captain (13th Rifle Brigade), later C.O. 8th Somersets.
[8] Lt. Col Challener, C.B., C.M.G., D.S.O., Commander 63rd Infantry Brigade, letter to Mary Hardy, 1919, *ibid.*
[9] Citation for Distinguished Service Order, *London Gazette,* 7th March, 1918.
[10] Vallings, *ibid.*
[11] Gough, *The Fifth Army,* Hodder & Stoughton, 1931, p.205.
[12] Colonel Repington, *The First World War, 1914-1918,* Vol. ii, pp.30-31. Constable, 1920.
[13] Vallings, *ibid.*
[14] *Ibid.*
[15] B. H. Liddell Hart, *History of the First World War* (1930) Cassell & Co., London.
[16] Lt. Col. A. T. Hitch, D.S.O., letter to Mary Hardy, 1919, *ibid.*
[17] Challener, *ibid.*
[18] Sheringham, *ibid.* Also Letter from Private Maurice Calvert to his father:

'When one Battalion relieves another in the line, the out-going officer hands the Padre over to the incoming officer as 'trench stores'; that is, a permanent trench fixture.'

Mary Hardy, *ibid*

[19] Sgt. Major R. Yaw, D.C.M., Letter to Mary Hardy, 1919, *ibid.*
[20] Watson, *ibid.*
[21] Hitch, *ibid.*

WAITING FOR A BOY TO LIVE
ROSSIGNOL WOOD, 5th APRIL, 1918

He was by himself now, the others had gone on and left him. His leg had felt numb at first, but by God it hurt and throbbed now — that is if you could call it a leg any more. His blood was mixing with the chalky mud — rather strange, he thought, just like putting jam in rice pudding at school. School, now there's a thought, they'll be putting up the cricket nets again in Taunton. He'd wondered what it would be like to die, now he expected to find out, and truth to tell he didn't really mind. He felt very cold. He'd lain there since six o'clock in the morning, stuck in the wire.

'It's only me. Keep quiet and still. They're back in the pill box again.'

He felt a tightening round his thigh as something was tied round it. Oh, my God, it throbs. He felt an arm round his shoulder and a coat being put over him.

* * * * *

He must have been unconscious because it was nearly dark again.

'Ssh . . . Keep still. It's only me. I'm still here.'

He knew that voice. It was the Padre, dear old Hardy. They talked in whispers. Rossignol Wood, it was called, a place for nightingales, but not tonight. The old man told him how he used to go down to the Oval to watch W.G. bat when he was a schoolboy. Did he play cricket at school, the old man asked. Yes, but the summer of 1917 seemed a long time ago. He didn't suppose he'd ever play cricket again with a leg like this. Course you will, said the old man, anyway you can't do worse than me . . . I always got a duck. Oh God, God, God it hurts . . . his teeth chattered and his body was shaking. He could hear the Germans talking and laughing in the pill box. They must have thought he was dead because they were only ten yards away. He couldn't understand what they said . . . only did Latin and Greek at school . . . Amo, Amas, Amat, Amamis, Amatis . . . .

'Keep quite still. I'm going to get help. I'll be back soon. You've done really well. Just hang on a bit longer.'

He felt the arm lift off his back, and the warmth of the old man's body go away from him. Oh, God it hurts, come back quickly.

He knew the old man would come back, that nothing, absolutely nothing, could stop him. Yes, he'd try to hang on a bit longer.

They did come back for him, the dear old padre and a tough old sergeant, both old enough to be his father. He knew what the Padre would say before he said it, 'It's only me.' The sergeant snipped the wire with his cutters, deadening the sound with a cloth.

It was like being a child again being carried back by these two old men. He'd tried to be brave, he really had. Then he couldn't remember any more.

* * * * *

He heard the sergeant got a D.C.M. Later, he heard that when the Colonel told the Padre he was to get the V.C., Hardy had replied, 'I really must protest.'

FOR VALOUR: THE VICTORIA CROSS

'What is courage but the inspiration of the Spirit.'

T. B. Hardy, July, 1918.

On 21st March, 1918, the German Army made its supreme effort to win the War. The 'Kaiserschlact' (the Kaiser's battle) was one of the great turning points of the War, and involved more men than any other battle. The German survivors had stamped in their Military Service Book: 'Grosse Schlacht in Frankerich' — 'The Great Battle in France'.

Like the British offensive in the summer of 1916, the German attack came to the south of the British line in the area of the Somme.

The collapse of Russia in 1917 had allowed Germany to transfer all her forces to the Western Front, allowing them to have a superiority in numbers for the first time since the Autumn of 1914. Ludendorff and the German High Command planned the attack with the greatest care and in the minutest detail. Their tactics were new and revolutionary, heralding the 'Blitzkreig' of 1940, and were remarkably effective. Strongpoints and areas of heavy resistance were to be by-passed and 'mopped-up' later; the line of least resistance was to be pursued and exploited. For the first time, the word 'stormtrooper' came into the language of warfare.

The attack dealt a devastating blow to the British, particularly to the 5th Army holding the most thinly defended part of the line to the South. For a few days it appeared as if the British Army could be defeated.

The 8th Lincolns, 8th Somersets and 4th Middlesex in the 63rd Brigade were rushed south by bus and train from Ypres, arriving at Gommecourt at the northern end of the Somme on 1st April.[1]

By this time Gough had been relieved of his command of the 5th Army, and the British were fighting a desperate rearguard action.[2] All the gains, and more, of 1916 had been lost, and the Lincolns found themselves in trenches last used nearly two years before.

The German effort ended on 5th April. They had gained over 1,000 square miles of territory and inflicted 160,000 casualties on the British (22,000 killed, 63,000 wounded, and 75,000 prisoners of war).[3]

The final German effort was made in the Northern Somme, the area in part defended by the 8th Lincolns and 8th Somersets (the 4th Middlesex were in reserve). As the Germans were forming up ready for this thrust, it was decided that the 37th Division (including the Lincolns and Somersets) should take part in a local pre-emptive strike in order to disorganise the enemy's attack. The strike was to take place early on the morning of the 5th April, and Theodore Hardy was to play such a full part in events that day that he was to receive his first (of four) recommendations for the Victoria Cross.

The Official History of the Lincolnshire Regiment records details of the two battalions' attack:

65

GERMAN OFFENSIVE
March 1918

Original line – March 21

Line on evening March 21

Line on evening March 23

Line on evening March 25

Line on evening April 5

0   5   10   15   20
Miles

The Somme area

The 8th Lincolns and 8th Somersets arrived in Gommecourt from Flanders on 1st April, 1918.

Theodore Hardy was awarded the Victoria Cross for four separate incidents, all involving rescuing the wounded, in Rossignol Wood on 5th April, and in Bucquoy on 25th, 26th and 27th April.

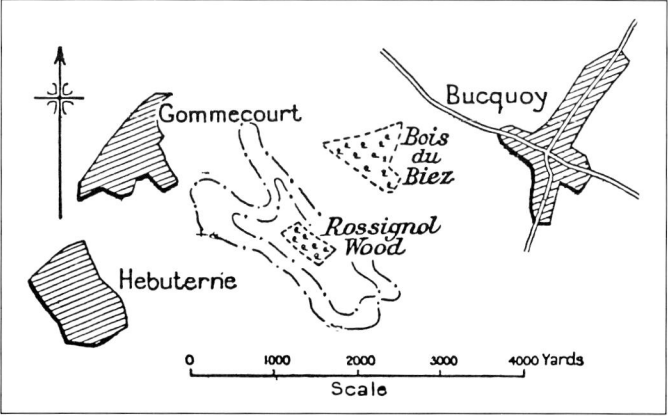

'On the 3rd April orders were issued for an attack on Rossignol Wood and the enemy's trenches west and south of it, the final objective being a sunken road south-west of the Wood and a short length of trench running eastwards from the eastern end of the Wood. This entailed on the Lincolnshire front the capture of Duck, Swan and Owl Trenches: Rossignol Wood, with Fish Alley and Roach Trench were in the area of the Somerset attack.

The night of the 4th/5th April was miserable in the extreme: rain fell and the inky darkness made the forming up operations difficult. . . . Tanks had been detailed to assist in the attack, but they were unable to advance. At zero hour (5.30 a.m.) therefore, the Lincolnshire advanced without their assistance.

Within fifty yards of the jumping-off line the right section suffered severely from machine gun fire, and a similar experience befell the left platoon. Considerable resistance from the first objective (Duck Trench) met the attackers, and heavy fighting took place during which about one hundred Germans were taken prisoner and from sixty to ninety wounded. This objective was captured by 5.45 a.m.

Considerable machine-gun fire from both flanks met the attack on the second objective (Swan Trench) . . . Having captured this line, heavy bombing became general on the right. The line was cleared with the exception of two strong points . . . and at 7.45 a.m. this position was being consolidated.

At about 9.00 a.m., lorries full of enemy troops were seen travelling towards Rossignol Wood, but the Lincolnshire still maintained their position. At midday the enemy was reinforced and the position of the battalion was likely to become serious.

At about 1.00 p.m. the enemy advanced and cut right into the battalion dividing it into two sections. "From this time", the record states, "we were overwhelmed and, owing to the lack of bombs, we withdrew in good order into our original front line".'[4]

As the battalions re-grouped and counted heads in their original line, there was no sign of Theodore Hardy. The Padre was missing.

As dusk approached and speculation grew that the man they had called 'the unkillable' would not be returning, a small figure was seen coming out of the wood from amongst the enemy lines. He had spent the day lying within ten yards of an enemy machine-gun post comforting a wounded man and now had come back to ask for a volunteer to go with him to recover the man.

A sergeant promptly agreed to return into Rossignol Wood with Theodore Hardy, and they crawled in silence to where the man lay. Although the man was too weak to stand, the sergeant and the Chaplain somehow managed to get him back to the safety of the Somersets' trench. Despite this ordeal, Hardy would not rest, as the citation continues:

'Throughout the day the enemy's artillery, machine-gun and trench-mortar fire was continuous, and caused many casualties. Notwithstanding, this very gallant chaplain was seen moving quietly amongst the men and tending the wounded, absolutely regardless of his personal safety'.[5]

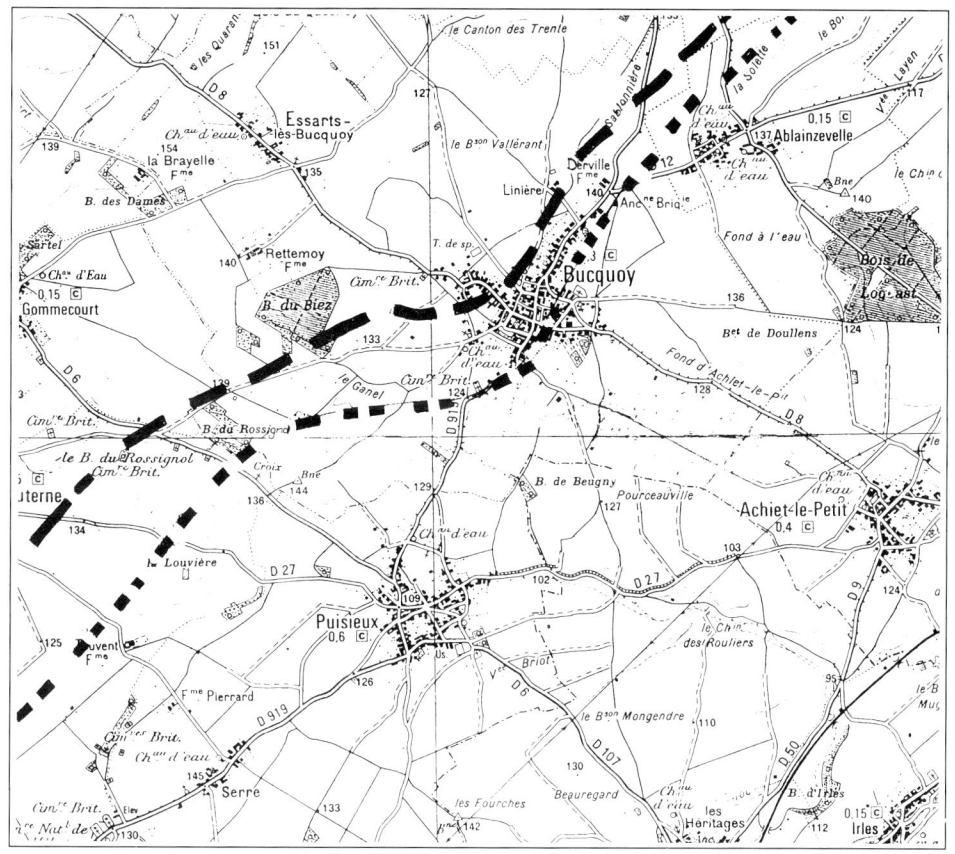

ROSSIGNOL WOOD AND BUCQUOY

The area where Theodore Hardy won his Victoria Cross has changed but little over the years.

Rossignol Wood still stands and the trees have now recovered. Wood anemones and cowslips grow in profusion in the wood. The German Pill Box where Hardy stayed all day on the wire can still be found in the remains of the German trenches running along the south eastern edge of the wood. Piles of rusty old shells are dumped on the edge of the road by farmers during their ploughing, and it is still possible to turn up bullets and bits of barbed wire in the fields round about.

It was in Achiet-le-Petit that Hardy was told of his appointment to be a Chaplain to the King.

The villages have now been rebuilt.

A permanent and sad reminder today are the numerous War Cemeteries shown on the map.

Bucquoy, northern Somme area. Hardy's citation for the Victoria Cross includes mention of digging wounded out of a collapsing building in Bucquoy during the great German offensive in April 1918.

The Brigadier, in his report on the day's events wrote: 'I consider that the behaviour of these battalions, which were composed largely of very young soldiers, was beyond all praise'. The Lincolns suffered 180 casualties, and the Somersets 161. The Sergeant who assisted Theodore Hardy was awarded the Distinguished Conduct Medal (Sergeant G. Radford) and other awards of the D.S.O., M.C., and D.C.M. were made.[6]

* * * * *

It was in the award of these other medals, that the Commander of the 37th division, Major-General Bruce-Williams, began to put together the facts leading to Theodore Hardy's award:

'I met Mr. Hardy walking back from the trenches and hailed him, and I asked him whether he could give me evidence regarding acts of gallantry by N.C.O.'s and men during the counter-attack on April 5th, which finally stemmed the Germans' attempt to push their advantage after the British retreat to the Hebuterne-Bucquoy line.

"He told me of several incidents, and I got him to name the men, and say what he saw them do. Having got the names out of him — he was always enthusiastic in his praise of the rank and file — I went then to interview the men whose names he had mentioned. Gradually out of these men I obtained and pieced together a story which proved that he, and nothing else, was really the inspiring spirit during a very hot period when the enemy's shelling was heavy to a degree. Then I made it my business to get the various statements recorded, and to see that they confirmed each other. The result was a V.C. for the Chaplain, who really *deserved it three times over*. I don't think Mr. Hardy ever realised that it was only out of his own mouth that I was able at last to get at the true facts of the case. For all the time he was so enthusiastic about the way other men behaved, and so keen that *their* gallantry should be recognised. Theirs was *nothing* to his."[7]

The facts collected by General Williams included events at Bucquoy later in the month as well as the rescue on the 5th April.

Although the main German effort was now transferred further north to Lens and to Flanders, the Gommecourt, Hebuterne and Bucquoy sector continued to be a most uncomfortable and difficult part of the line. Three more events took place on the 25th, 26th and 27th April in or near the ruined village of Bucquoy, and all resulted in the saving of life:

'An infantry.patrol had gone out to attack a previously located enemy post in the ruins of a village, the Reverend T. B. Hardy being then at Company Headquarters. Hearing firing, he followed the patrol, and about 400 yards beyond our front line of posts found an officer of the patrol dangerously wounded. He remained with the officer until he was able to get assistance to bring him in. During this time there was a great deal of firing, and an enemy patrol actually penetrated between the spot at which the officer was lying and our front line and captured three of our men.' [8]

K.S.R. 1915 1017 5000×200

No. G. 14.

EGYPTIAN STATE TELEGRAPHS مصلحة التلغرافات المصريه

No. نمرة 54 | Orig'l No. نمرة اصليه 2649 | Words كلمات 21

RECEIVED ورد — From 9D — At الساعه 1 24 — By التلغرافجي

SENT الارسل — To ال — At الساعه — By التلغرافجي

Date Stamp ختم المكتب

To الى Capt W. H. Hardy
R A M C 26
Stationary Hospital
Ismailia

REMARKS ملحوظات V.E Efm Par Abdallah

Office of Origin مكتب التصدير Dunkerque | Date تاريخ 6 | Time وقت 4 4.5p

father awarded D.S.O. no details yet
Hardy

EGYPTIAN STATE TELEGRAPHS مصلحة التلغرافات المصريه

No. نمرة 54 | Orig'l No. نمرة اصليه 120 | Words كلمات 17

RECEIVED ورد — From من 9D — At الساعه 1 31 — By التلغرافجي

SENT الارسل — To ال — At الساعه — By التلغرافجي

Date Stamp ختم المكتب

To الى Captain W H Hardy
R A M C 26 Stationary
Hospital Ismailia

REMARKS ملحوظات V.E Efm

Office of Origin مكتب التصدير France | Date تاريخ 13 | Time وقت 10 15A

father awarded V.C.
Hardy

This description of the event is taken from the V.C. citation. Colonel Challener added details when he wrote to Mary Hardy:

> 'He followed an officer's night patrol without anyone being aware of the fact. This patrol was attacked, the officer was so seriously wounded that he probably would have bled to death. Fortunately for him, Mr. Hardy found him in the dark, and using his knife cord as a tourniquet, stopped the bleeding and got him into our lines safely.' [9]

The next day Theodore Hardy saved more human life, again let us use the citation to describe the event in Bucquoy:

> 'When an enemy shell exploded in the middle of one of our posts, the Reverend T. B. Hardy at once made his way to the spot, despite the shell and trench-mortar fire which was going on at the time, and set to work to extricate the buried men. He succeeded in getting out one man who had been completely buried. He then set to work to extricate a second man, who was found to be dead.
>
> During the whole of the time that he was digging out the men this chaplain was in great danger, not only from shell fire, but also because of the dangerous condition of the wall of the building which had been hit by the shell which buried the men.' [10]

Sergeant-Major Yaw was an eye-witness and vividly describes the scene:

> "I remember him on one occasion; my company was holding the line, and the shelling was rather heavy; one of the posts, which was an old house, got blown in, and the men inside were buried underneath. Who should be first there but Mr. Hardy, who had already got some of them out by digging with his hands. I am sorry to say one poor fellow had to be left under the debris, having already been killed by the fall, and it was impossible to shift the other stuff, as the surrounding walls would have collapsed. Captain Hardy read the Funeral Service where he saved the others who would have been suffocated had he not been there, doing the work he loved, visiting the men.' [11]

The photograph in this chapter shows the condition of Bucquoy at this time. The C.O. of the 8th Lincolns remembered how difficult and dangerous the village was, and the part played by Hardy in the following weeks,

> 'We were holding a part of the line which ran through the ruined village of Bucquoy — half the village was in our hands and half in German hands — and owing to the ruins of houses everywhere, it was an impossible task to construct anything in the way of a continuous trench. Our line consequently consisted of a series of posts garrisoned by about seven men each and lying, roughly, a hundred or a hundred and fifty yards apart; these posts were naturally made as inconspicuous as possible, and the location of these posts at night when visiting the men was a matter of the greatest difficulty owing to the ground between and all around them being a wilderness of ruined houses, hedges, fallen trees, and so on.

And yet when visiting these posts, we always met the Padre, either lying in a post chatting in undertones to the men, or making his way from one post to the next. He was more often than not by himself, although the Boche was at that time quite enterprising, and would attempt to crawl round and rush one of the posts quite frequently.

During this time, the Padre would not live at Company Headquarters, which was a few hundred yards behind the post line, but insisted on living at advanced Platoon Headquarters, which was in an old German dug-out about thirty yards behind the actual post line, and in a neighbourhood where trench mortar shells occasionally made things very unpleasant. It was the constant sharing of danger and hardships in the line which gave him his tremendous power with the men — a power he would never realise himself — and which endeared him so to us all.'[12]

On the 11th July, it was formally announced in The London Gazette that the Reverend Theodore Bayley Hardy, D.S.O., M.C., Temporary Chaplain to the Forces 4th Class, had been awarded the Victoria Cross. The consensus of opinion in the two Battalions was that, 'he should have had it served up for breakfast every day'.

Elizabeth had no sooner sent a telegram — 'Father awarded the V.C.' — to William in Alexandria, than she received an invitation to visit 3rd Army Headquarters at Frohen-le-Grande on 9th August. The King himself was to present her father with the supreme award, and she was to witness the ceremony:

'It was to be a quiet and informal investiture. Father's V.C. was the first given. He had to stand in front of the King for about ten minutes listening to a full account of his deeds, looking perfectly miserable. A cinema apparatus was focussed on him all the time. He will appear in the London Picture House looking just like a schoolboy being scolded.

Then the King put on him the Great Medal, and I was near enough to him to hear quite distinctly as he spoke general appreciative sentences; you can fancy how I felt all the time.' [13]

Elizabeth's warmth and pride in her 'naughty schoolboy' father shine through her account of the day. This same warmth and pride can be seen as she watches on in the official photograph of the occasion.

The results of the 'Cinema apparatus' have proved remarkably elusive, almost as if Hardy himself was trying to cover up his decorations again. The Imperial War Museum did indeed have film of the King's visit to France between 5th and 13th August. There is film of the King on the 5th, 6th, 7th, 8th, 10th, 11th, 12th and 13th August; all catalogued with detailed descriptions, but of the 9th August — nothing! [14]

Nothing, that is, until at the very end of the catalogue comes the bare description, 'Summary, see also reel 99, which consists of out-takes and additional material of the visit.' The film library curator kindly agreed to view these odds and ends — and found exactly four seconds of the King talking to Theodore Hardy and six seconds to Elizabeth. To the best of the author's knowledge this brief four seconds is the only moving picture record of T. B. Hardy.

H.M. King George V presents Theodore Hardy with the Victoria Cross.
3rd Army Headquarters, Frohen-le-Grande, 9th August, 1918. Elizabeth Hardy stands in the background.

Almost fifty years later, Elizabeth was to re-live this day when her father's medals were presented to the Royal Army Chaplains' Department on permanent loan. She also unveiled a painting of the scene by Terence Cuneo. [15] A photograph of the occasion appeared in the 'Daily Telegraph' on 1st June, 1967, and produced a number of letters from old comrades. Fred Mott, of the 8th Somersets remembered his 'gallant and beloved Chaplain' returning with the V.C. to find the battalion assembled in a barn at Souastre ready to greet and cheer him — much to Mr. Hardy's astonishment and embarrassment. Mr. Mott:

> 'has always remembered the way, when the Rev. Hardy left the barn, he held his hand over the decoration, and blessed a photograph of (the Private's) Baby son.' [16]

The welcome in the barn at Souastre was held on 17th August and was to be a bitter sweet memory. The moving spirit who organised it was the C.O. of the 8th Somersets, Lt.-Colonel J.H.M. Hardyman. Just six days earlier his conduct during a German attack was to earn him the D.S.O.; seven days later Hardyman was killed during the British Offensive when he was yet again leading from the front. [17] Theodore Hardy himself had just two more months to live.

Miss Elizabeth Hardy, 80, with medals awarded to her late father, the Rev. Theodore Bayley Hardy, standing beside a painting showing King George V decorating him with the Victoria Cross in France in 1918. Miss Hardy appears as a Red Cross nurse in the Terence Cuneo painting, which was unveiled yesterday at the Royal Army Chaplains' Department Depot, Bagshot, Surrey.

Photograph in the 'Daily Telegraph,' 1st June, 1967.

Cuneo's painting contains a certain amount of dramatic licence. 3rd Army Headquarters at Frohen-le-Grande was well behind the front line and never suffered shell damage. Nor did Hardy wear a helmet at the investiture.

Elizabeth herself was to have a remarkable life. She was a graduate of London University when very few women went on to further education. After her father's death, she had to leave the Red Cross and was obliged to take up a teaching post, presumably for financial reasons.

She went on to become Headmistress of a Girls' Secondary School in Rangoon. During World War II she drove through Burma to India narrowly escaping capture by the Japanese. She then became Head of a School in Bangalore before retiring to Cornwall.

In September, 1965, the Hardy family presented the Padre's medals to the Royal Army Chaplains' Department at Bagshot on permanent loan.

William became a much loved General Practitioner in Croydon. His daughter, Patricia Hastings Hardy, is now Secretary to the Archbishop of Dublin, Church of Ireland. Patricia is now Theodore Hardy's only living descendant. In April, 1988, she presented her Grandfather's New Testament to the Chaplains' Department.

Reverend Theodore Bayley Hardy, D.S.O., M.C.
T/C.F. 4th Class, Army Chaplains' Department.
Attached 8th Battalion, Lincolnshire Regiment

'For most conspicuous bravery and devotion to duty on many occasions. Although over 50 years of age he has, by his fearlessness, devotion to men of his battalion and quiet, unobtrusive manner, won the respect and admiration of the whole division.

His marvellous energy and endurance would be remarkable even in a very much younger man and his valour and devotion are exemplified in the following incidents:

An infantry patrol had gone out to attack a previously located enemy post in the ruins of a village, the Reverend Theodore Bayley Hardy, C.F., being then at company headquarters. Hearing firing, he followed the patrol and about 400 yards beyond our front line of posts, found an officer of the patrol dangerously wounded. He remained with the officer until he was able to get assistance to bring him in. During this time there was a great deal of firing and an enemy patrol actually penetrated betwen the spot at which the officer was lying and our front line and captured three of our men.

On a second occasion when an enemy shell exploded in the middle of one of our posts, the Reverend T.B. Hardy at once made his way to the spot, despite shell and trench mortar fire which were going on at the time and set to work to extricate the buried men. He succeeded in getting out one man who had been completely buried. He then set to work to extricate a second man who was found to be dead.

During the whole of the time that he was digging out the men this chaplain was in great danger not only from shell fire but also because of the dangerous condition of the wall of the building, which had been hit by the shell which buried the men.

On a third occasion he displayed the greatest devotion to duty when our infantry, after a successful attack, were gradually forced back to their starting trench.

After it was believed that all our men had withdrawn from the wood Chaplain Hardy came out of it and on reaching the advanced post, asked the men to help him to get in a wounded man. Accompanied by a sergeant, he made his way to the spot where the man lay, within 10 yards of a pill-box which had been captured in the morning, but was subsequently recaptured and occupied by the enemy. The wounded man was too weak to stand, but between them the chaplain and the sergeant eventually succeeded in getting him to our lines.

Throughout the day the enemy's artillery, machine-gun and trench mortar fire was continuous and caused many casualties.

Notwithstanding, this very gallant chaplain was soon moving quietly amongst the men and tending the wounded absolutely regardless of his personal safety.'

Dates of Acts of Bravery	*London Gazette*
5-25-26-27th April, 1918	11th July, 1918

Citation for the award of the Victoria Cross

[1] War Diary, 8th Battalion, Lincolnshire Regiment.
In the February, 1918 re-organisation, many Brigades were reduced to three battalions. Thus, the 10th Yorks & Lancs left 63rd Brigade.

[2] See, Middlebrook, 'The Kaiser's Battle, 21st March, 1918: The First Day of the German Spring Offensive,' Allen Lane, London, 1978.
It is generally held now, that Gough was unfairly dismissed and treated as a scapegoat for the inadequacies and bad planning of others. The weakness of the 5th Army was due more to the feud between Haig and Lloyd George than to any failure on Gough's part.

[3] Middlebrook, op. cit. p.347.

[4] Op. cit.

[5] *London Gazette*, 11th July, 1918. Citation for Victoria Cross, extract.

[6] History of the Somerset Light Infantry, op. cit. p.290.

[7] Letter to Mary Hardy, 1919.

[8] *London Gazette*, ibid.

[9] Letter to Mary Hardy, 1919.

[10] *London Gazette*, ibid.

[11] Letter to Mary Hardy, 1919.

[12] Ibid.

[13] Elizabeth Hardy, letter to Mary Hardy, August, 1918.

[14] The gap is interesting in another sense. The King and the General Staff were anxiously awaiting news of the first day of the British counter-attack, following the final German offensive in July.

[15] Painting in Chapel of Royal Army Chaplains' Department, Bagshot.
There is a certain amount of poetic licence in an otherwise remarkable painting. Hardy is shown wearing a tin helmet instead of his cap, and the Chateau is shown to have shell damage on the left. It was, in fact, well behind the lines and far away from any danger.

[16] Letter to Archdeacon I. D. Neill from Mrs. Joy Mott, 20th September, 1965.

[17] Details of Hardyman's award and death on pp307/309, *History of the Somerset Light Infantry*, op. cit.
According to Bishop Gwynne, when Colonel Hardyman first told Theodore Hardy of the recommendation for the Victoria Cross,' Hardy protested.

'I knew nothing of what was going on in No-Man's Land while I was attending to an officer who had been seriously wounded on the wire entanglements. I really think I ought to put in a protest.'

Hardyman wisely replied: "All right, Padre, but if you do you will only be advertising yourself all the more."

Hardy reluctantly accepted this and allowed the recommendation to go forward.

Jackson, op. cit. p.159

Hardyman was a very gallant officer, rising in just over a year from the rank of Lieutenant to Lieutenant-Colonel. He was with the 8th Somersets throughout the time Theodore Hardy was with them until his own death. According to the official record he had an inspiring presence in the Battalion when many of the troops were 'only boys who had seen little or no previous service'. In addition to the D.S.O., he was twice Mentioned in Despatches, and was awarded the M.C. after the death of Colonel Scott at Arras.

MR. VALIANT-FOR-TRUTH

'For if the trumpet give an <u>uncertain sound</u>, who shall prepare himself to the battle.'

(I Corinthians 14.8)

marked by T. B. Hardy in his pocket New Testament.

Wherever Theodore Hardy went . . . Arras, the mud of Passchendaele, Rossignol Wood, the bridge at Briastre, and finally Rouen . . . a battered little red book went with him. It was his pocket New Testament, and one can see the bulge of it below the medal ribbons in his studio portrait. It now rests in the Chaplains' Department at Bagshot. [1]

In it, he marked certain passages and made brief notes. One is struck by how few markings there are, and this must make those passages and words that are marked all the more significant. To handle and read through this little book is to come close to Hardy: to glimpse his inner thoughts, to see what his ministry meant to him, and to feel the source of his inspiration.

Passages are marked which would be read to confirmation candidates in shell holes and outposts. The poor soul slowly drowning in the mud at Oostaverne, the wounded and dying in the dressing stations, a bereaved soldier grieving for a comrade, all would hear words of comfort from this book. One can imagine Hardy drawing consolation and fresh strength in a brief moment of solitude resting in a dug-out before his nocturnal visits to the front line outposts. It is not too fanciful to see him marking a passage by flickering candle-light as he, 'listened to the roar, Of the guns that hammered Thiepval, Like big breakers on the shore.' [2]

'I speak as to wise men; judge ye what I say' is marked in I Corinthians 10.15. The young men around Hardy had experience of life and death in extremis more profound than any previous generation. Most had little education, and before the War probably led a life limited to their own area. Yet they had now seen death, horror, fear, courage and the very highest comradeship as exemplified by Private Thomas Sage, V.C. of the 8th Somersets.

Here, then was a true communion of souls with wisdom based not on intellect or age but on common experience and comradeship. Thus, we find . . .

> 'for none of us liveth to himself, and no man dieth to himself' (Romans 14.7)
> 'We are all the children of the light' (Thessalonians 5.5)
> 'but Christ <u>is</u> all, and in all' (Colossians 4.11)
> 'And be at peace among yourselves. Now we exhort you, brethren, warn them that are unruly, comfort the feeble minded, support the weak, be patient toward all men' (I Thessalonians 13.14)
> 'He that spared not his own son, but delivered him up <u>for us all</u>' (Romans 8.32)

For Hardy, there was a natural linkage between the communion of comradeship to the Act of Communion itself. Geoffrey Vallings recalled that Hardy held:

'And Jesus said unto them, I am the bread of life: he that cometh to me shall never hunger; and he that believeth in me shall never thirst' (St. John 6.35).
Passage marked by T. B. Hardy in his pocket New Testament

(Photo — Imperial War Museum)

'a fixed idea, that our preparation for confirmation was far too long. Not that he neglected it when opportunity offered, but I have known him present men with what some of my reverend brethren would call no preparation at all. But then we are not all Hardys, and it was the personality of the man which enabled him to do more for a human soul by a few minutes' contact than most of us could do during months of instruction.' [3]

The 'few minutes contact' must have been simple and direct. A series of markings in Matthew's Gospel are almost all at points where Jesus is declared to be 'the Son of God' (often this phrase alone is underlined). It may be that this reflects the current questioning of Jesus's divinity, and is an answer to the common assertion at that time that Jesus was simply a 'good man.'

What Jesus meant to Hardy comes from his annotations in John's Gospel. For Hardy God was a God of love and mercy, and Jesus was the agent of salvation. The so called 'comfortable words' are marked and underlined:

'For God so loved the world, that he gave his only begotten son, that whosoever believeth in him should not perish, but have everlasting life.
For God sent not his Son into the world to condemn the world; but that the world through him might be saved.' (John 3.16/17)

Then there is John 6.51, 53-58, where Jesus speaks of himself as 'the living bread' and where he promises his presence now and resurrection and eternal life to those who eat this bread. The very ordinary act of receiving Communion takes on a new dimension in the mud and squalor of the trenches when those receiving it are living perpetually under the shadow of death, and these words reinforce that.

We know that Hardy had difficulty with the damnatory clauses in the Athanasian creed, and his cousin Bessie Hardy remembered:

'A habit of his was: whenever the Psalms for the day were of a vindictive character, he would give a few explanatory notes, before his sermon, showing the difference under the Christian Dispensation. The great truth he always emphasised was God's unlimited love for man.' [4]

In Chapter One of Romans, St. Paul lists a long catalogue of sins — yet Hardy underlines but one — 'unmerciful'.

With the themes of love and mercy goes reconciliation. The enemy was not to be hated:

'Therefore if thou bring thy gift to the altar, and there rememberest that thy brother hath ought against thee;
Leave there thy gift before the altar, and go thy way; first be reconciled to thy brother, and then come and offer thy gift.' (Matthew 5.23/24)

There are echoes here of Studdert-Kennedy who refused to serve with one officer who kept telling the men that the way to win the war was to kill as many Germans as possible. The Deputy Chaplain General, Bishop Gwynne, recalled how most of the troops defied these instructions and Studdert-Kennedy was delighted to hear some Londoners boast that they took more prisoners than any other unit in the British Army. [5]

Maybe this message got through to a sergeant in the 8th Lincolns who stopped Private Jimmy Watson from bayoneting a German with the words, "Stop, Jim. He's some mother's son." [6]

'For all the law is fulfilled in one word, even in this;
Thou shalt love thy neighbour as thyself.' (Galatians 5.14)

Whilst in James 1.19 is marked,

'. . . let every man be swift to hear, slow to speak, slow to wrath.'

Aggression and fear were two aspects of psychological stress induced by the War. Shell shock, with men shaking from head to foot and unable to move, was a new and little understood problem. Norman Gladden went through the Flanders campaign and described two such cases:

'A salvo fell venomously across the path ahead of us . . . A (man) was severely shell shocked; he reeled back towards the sap like one pleasantly tipsy, quite incapable of controlling his reactions.' [7]

Later he describes a regular soldier who had served since 1914:

'A Mons man, a smart soldier and in every way an estimable person . . . a shell salvo turned him into an incoherent and gesticulating figure. Previous cases that I had seen had been anonymous to me, and although shocking enough in all senses none had had the impact of this incident which involved someone I knew and respected.' [8]

Was Hardy thinking of men such as these when he marked the following passages?

'When the even was come, they brought unto him many that were possessed with devils: and he cast out the spirits with his word, and healed all that were sick." (Matthew 8.16)

'But if I cast out devils by the spirit of God, then the Kingdom of God is come unto you.' (Matthew 12.28)

How much Hardy, or anyone else at that time, knew about shell-shock it is difficult to say. He was no doubt struggling to understand it and to cope with it, and his response was probably instinctive.

Yet it is not unreasonable to believe that his quiet re-assuring presence in the aftermath of such an incident did indeed help to salvage men in this condition. Support for this view comes from the leading modern authority on such cases:

> 'This reasoning is based upon understanding the psychiatric casualty and how such cases should be handled . . . With every step a soldier takes towards the relative safety of some rearward area the harder it becomes to cure the disability . . . Men who have received any Christian teaching at their mothers' knees, and even those who have not, do tend to call upon God when afraid in battle.' [9]

By being at the front Hardy was in the right place to help, and his calm quiet familiar strength would give an immediate anchor to such cases.

Even more difficult is the perennial question of how an omnipotent God could allow such a terrible event ast the First World War to take place. We know from his sister-in-law's writings that Hardy did not ignore this point. For Hardy, God identified with suffering, and indeed through Christ had suffered Himself.

Mary Hardy tells us that he was fully alive to the fact that life is full of problems which no reason can solve, and mysteries of which we have no explanation. He offered no facile or glib answers to these points. At the heart of it all was a mystery:

> 'O the depth of the riches both of the wisdom and knowledge of God! how unsearchable are his judgements, and his ways past finding out." (Romans 12.33)

Yet after the long Good Friday was the promise of Easter Day.

Death was an everpresent reality, part of Hardy's daily round. As Studdert-Kennedy wrote:

> 'All that week I'd buried brothers . . .' [7]

For Hardy, the promise of eternal life was a reality, Vallings tells us that Hardy:

> 'Looked upon his wife as alive with him, in constant communion and fellowship. He loved his children intensely, but he believed that he could do no better, if God so willed, than join his beloved wife in the presence of their Lord. Death, as many of us regard it, simply did not exist for him.' [8]

In Revelation 1.17 and 1.18 the three words . . . <u>Fear not</u> . . . <u>death</u> are underlined.

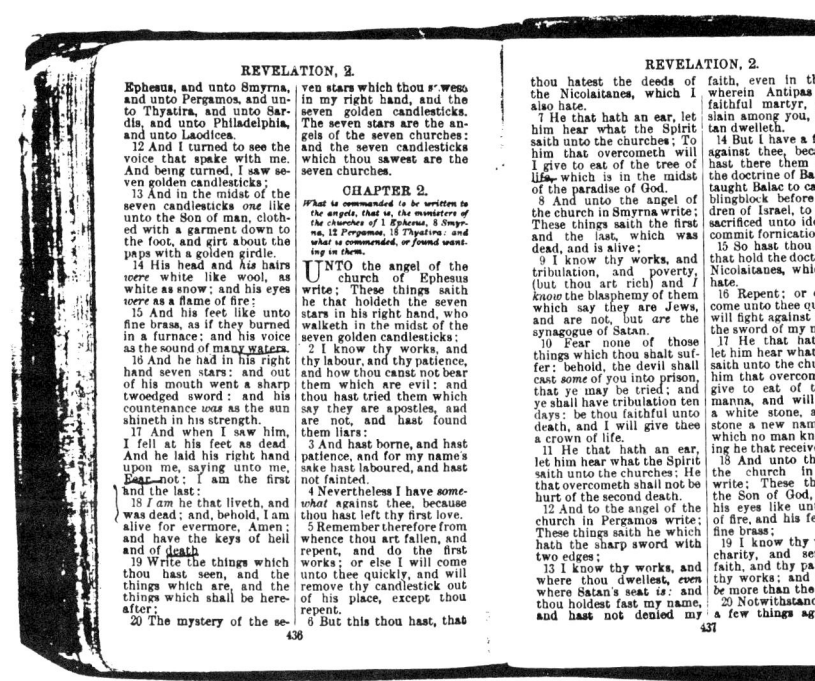

'Fear not . . . death'

Hardy must have known the burial service off by heart by the time he had been in the trenches a few weeks, and no doubt the long passage from I Corinthians 15, which forms the only set reading in the old Prayer Book. We know of his insistence on saying the Burial Service in the incidents at Oostaverne and Bucquoy. He stood to say the words despite being under enemy fire.

He chose to pick out those verses in which the Easter challenge is presented most forcibly: 'If in this life only we have hope in Christ, we are of all men most miserable. But now is Christ risen from the dead, and become the first fruits of them that slept. For since by man came death, by man came also the resurrection of the dead. For as in Adam all die, even so in Christ shall all be made alive." (I Corinthians 15.19 to 22.)

For those grieving and suffering, and no doubt to himself, he has marked two passages in St. John (the first with a very rare double mark)

'Ye shall know the truth, and the truth shall make you free.' (John 8.32)

And again:

'These things I have spoken unto you, that in me ye might have peace. In the world ye shall have tribulation: but be of good cheer: I have overcome the world.' John 16.33

Burial in the trenches

"There are many kinds of sorrow
In this world of Love and Hate,
But there is no sterner sorrow
Than a soldier's for his mate."

Geoffrey Studdert-Kennedy

"If in this life only we have hope in Christ, we are of all men most miserable.
But now is Christ risen from the dead, and become the first fruits of them that slept.
For since by man came death, by man came also the resurrection of the dead.
For as in Adam all die, even so in Christ shall all be made alive." (I Corinthians 15, 19-22)
Passage marked by T. B. Hardy in his pocket New Testament.

We also get glimpses of what Hardy's ministry meant to him. In II Timothy 4.5 he sets himself the challenge: 'make full proof of thy ministry.'

Part of that Ministry was to go where the vast majority of the Chaplains failed to go, the front line, 'I strived to preach the gospel, not where Christ was named.' (Romans 15.20)

In preaching this gospel he spoke of a loving and merciful God, and of the promise of salvation. But we are told that he did not ignore coarse language or behaviour, and behind the diffident shyness was an immensely strong character with a directness of speech when he felt the occasion merited it. The C.O. of the 8th Somersets tells us:

> 'His humble nature, his Christ-like personality were most remarkable. As a Minister of God he frequently hit hard; but he was always sympathetic, and while he never compromised with wrong, his addresses to the troops were typical of his natural humility, wherein lay his strength.' [9]

This strength through humility, and his natural sympathy for others is seen here:

> 'Am I therefore become your enemy, because I tell you the truth?' (Galatians 4.16)
> 'For in that he himself hath suffered being tempted, he is able to succour them that are tempted.' (Hebrews 2.18)

Strength through weakness, the paradox at the heart of Christianity, of Christ facing Pilate, had a special message for Hardy as he faced his own inner struggles of life in the trenches. He has marked a whole string of passages on this theme:

> 'He said unto me, My grace is sufficient for thee: for my strength is made perfect in weakness . . . for when I am weak, then am I strong.' (II Corinthians 12. 9,10)
> 'For we are glad when we are weak . . .' (II Corinthians 13.9)
> 'Who out of weakness were made strong, waxed valiant in the fight, turned to flight the armies of the aliens.' (Hebrews 11.34)

These texts take on a new depth when placed in the context of the daily fatigue, drudgery, discomfort and cold of trench life where everyone, including Hardy, faced the imminent possibility of wounds and death.

His first thought was for others. His faith gave him strength, and his strength must be used for others:

> 'Who comforteth us in all our tribulations, that we may be able to comfort them which are in any trouble, by the comfort wherewith we ourselves are comforted of God.' (II Corinthians 1.4)
> 'Therefore, my beloved brethren, be ye steadfast, unmoveable, always abounding in the work of the Lord, forasmuch as ye know that your labour is not in vain in the lord.' (I Corinthians 15.58)

'Your labour is not in vain in the Lord.' One must wonder if this phrase echoed round and round in Hardy's thoughts during the mind numbing slog carrying stretchers through the mud of Passchendaele. Amidst all the slaughter and carnage every single life was precious, to be cherished and to be striven for. As exhaustion and fatigue gripped him, and as his elderly body must have shrieked for rest, he was driven on because 'his labour was not in vain in the Lord'.

Studdert-Kennedy again finds the words for us in his poem 'to Stretcher-Bearers':

'Stick it, lad, ye'll soon be there now
Want to rest 'ere for a while?
Let 'im dahn then — gently — gently,
There ye are, lad. That's the style . . .
Ow's it goin' now then, sonny?
'Ere's that narrow bit o'trench,
Careful mate, there's some dead Jerries.
Gawd Almighty, what a stench!
'Ere we are now, stretcher case, boys,
Bring him aht a cup o' tea!
IN AS MUCH AS YE HAVE DONE IT
YE HAVE DONE IT UNTO ME.'

To read through Hardy's New Testament and to see his markings is to be taken on a spiritual journey whether one holds the Christian Faith or not. It is to follow in the footsteps of Mr. Valiant-for-truth as 'he steps out on his own Pilgrimage to follow his Master.

'Let us therefore come boldly unto the throne of grace, that we may obtain mercy, and find grace to help in time of need.' (Hebrews 4.16)

The 'steadfast' theme constantly recurs,

'He steadfastly set his face to go to Jerusalem . . .' Luke 9.51
(to the death that awaited him on the Cross)

There was to be no flinching or turning back:

'Jesus said unto him, No man having put his hand to the plough, and looking back is fit for the Kingdom of God.' (Luke 10.62)
'But we are not of them that draw back . . .' (Hebrews 10.39)
'And let us not be weary in well doing: for in due season we shall reap, if we faint not.' (Galatians 6.9)

Perhaps most revealing of all are a clutch of markings in Acts 20 — the only ones to come in the Book of Acts, which must make them all the more significant. Here in Paul's speech to the Elders at Ephesus as he stopped off on his journey to Jerusalem with all its forecasts of imprisonment and possible death we catch a glimpse of Hardy's inspiration:

'He hasted, if it were possible for him, to be at Jerusalem the day of Pentecost . . .

Serving the Lord with all humility of mind, and with many tears, and temptations, which befell me . . .

Testifying, repentence toward God, and faith to our Lord Jesus Christ . . .

But none of these things move me, neither count I my life dear unto myself, so that I might finish my course with joy, and the ministry, which I have received of the Lord Jesus, to testify the gospel of the grace of God." (Acts 20. 16,19,21,24)

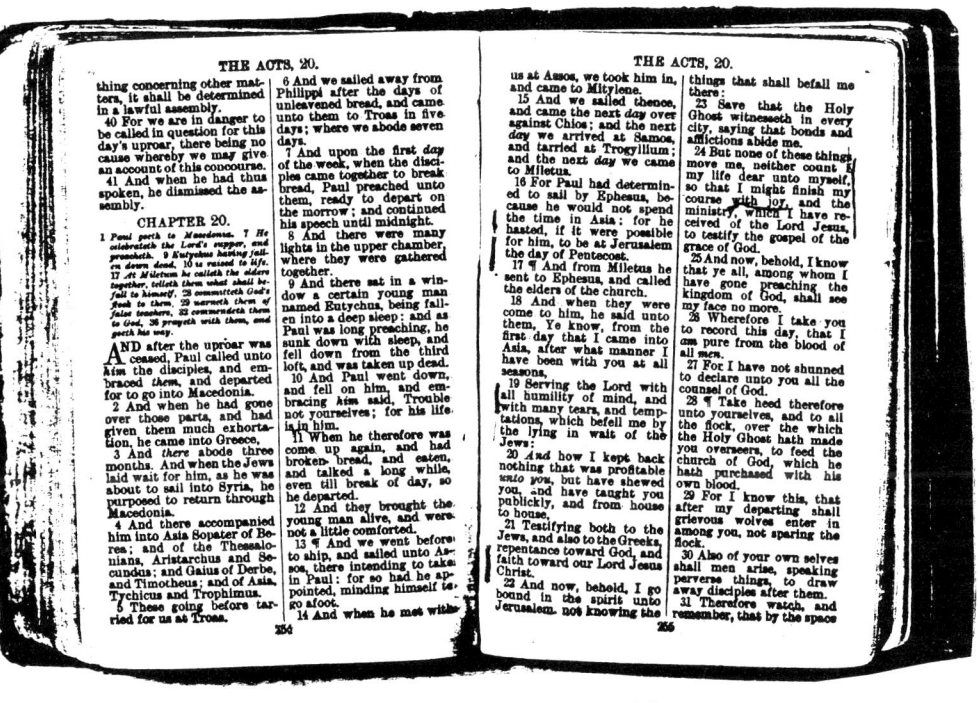

. . . so that I might finish my course with joy . . .

The last of Hardy's markings — and there are only four of them — appear at the end in the Book of Revelation. Two we have mentioned, *'Fear not . . . Death'*

The last two, he must have seen as the Lord's word to him in his prayers — a command to go through into the unknown; confirmation that his desperately sacrificial ministry was right; and commendation in just those words which his humble and unassuming nature would delight to accept:

'I know thy works: behold, I have set before thee an open door, and no man can shut it; for thou hast a little strength, and hast kept my word, and hast not denied my name.' (Revelations 3.8)

The last words come almost as a shout of triumph overwhelming the tumult and misery of war, and his own last journey on that plank bridge over the River Selle.

'And I heard as it were the voice of a great multitude, and as the voice of many waters, and as the voice of mighty thunderings, saying, Alleluia: for the Lord God omnipotent reigneth.' (Revelations 19.6)

[1] The New Testament was presented to the Chaplains Department on permanent loan by Miss Patricia Hastings Hardy in April, 1988.

[2] G. A. Studdert-Kennedy , 'His Mate' in, 'The Unutterable Beauty,' 1927, Mowbray.

[3] Vallings in Hardy, opus cit.

[4] Hardy, ibid.

[5] H. C. Jackson, 'Pastor of the Nile,' a life of Bishop L. H. Gwynne, Deputy Chaplain General, 1960, p.157.

[6] James Watson, interview with Author, 10th August, 1986.

[7] Gladden, opus cit.

[8] Ibid.

[9] Major General Frank Richardson C.B., D.S.O., O.B.E., M.D., medical postscript in a study of Capital Courts Martial, 1914-18, 'For the Sake of Example,' by His Honour Judge Anthony Babington, pp. 220/223. Leo Cooper, London, 1983.

[10] Studdert-Kennedy.

[11] Vallings, in Hardy, ibid.

[12] Sheringham, in Hardy, ibid.

[13] Studdert-Kennedy, 'To Stretcher Bearers,' ibid.

Author's Note.
I am especially grateful to Miss Patricia Hastings Hardy for allowing me to see her Grandfather's New Testament before she deposited it with the Chaplains' Department for safe keeping. I am also very grateful to Canon Michael Westropp for carefully and laboriously copying out Theodore Hardy's markings and annotations into an identical copy of the New Testament.
I am also very much indebted to the Bishop of Penrith for helping me to interpret the various passages, and for his very considerable help in other ways.

MR. VALIANT-FOR-TRUTH CROSSES THE RIVER

'So he passed over, and all the trumpets sounded for him on the other side.'
Pilgrim's Progress — John Bunyan

Throughout the Spring and early Summer of 1918 the Germans continued their effort for a decisive breakthrough. They drove deeply into British and French held territory, recapturing all the area in Flanders so dearly won by the British the previous Autumn. But the decisive victory never came, and in the process of attempting it the Germans exhausted themselves.

During this period the 8th Lincolns and 8th Somersets carried out a continual round of trench duty in the Bucquoy sector. Whenever they withdrew for a few days rest, the Padre would stay in the line with the relieving battalion (usually the 4th Middlesex, the 13th Rifle Brigade, the 2nd Canterbury (New Zealand), or the 5th King's Own Yorkshire Light Infantry). The usual pattern would be six days in the trenches, six days on working parties behind the line, and if they were lucky six days to rest and clean up equipment.

The final German effort came in mid-July to the East of Reims, but its success was minimal. The Germans had clearly shot their bolt, and by now the Allies were being re-inforced by 300,000 American troops a month. The tide was about to turn. The 8th August (the day before Hardy received his V.C.) was described by Ludendorff as 'Black Tuesday' when the British, Australians and Canadians advanced in the Somme.

"August 8th was the black day of the German Army in the history of the war . . . It put the decline of our fighting power beyond all doubt . . . The war must be ended."

Within three months it was.

* * * * *

When the 8th Somersets gathered in the barn at Souastre to greet and cheer their highly embarrassed Chaplain, for many it was to be the last time they would be together. With the 8th Lincolns they immediately moved into support positions ready to take part in the final offensive.

At 4.50 a.m. on 21st August the whistles blew and they climbed out of the trenches in heavy mist to attack Bucquoy. As usual a now much decorated non-combatant went with them.

Five days fierce fighting followed during which they advanced over six miles and captured Bapaume. The Lincolns suffered 177 casualties and the Somersets 170. Colonel Hardyman, the Somersets' C.O., was one of those killed. Hardy's friend Captain Madden was awarded the Military Cross, and Company Sergeant Major Yaw the Distinguished Conduct Medal.

The advance continued as other Brigades leapfrogged through, allowing the two battalions of Lincolns and Somersets to rest and recover at Achiet. It was whilst they were

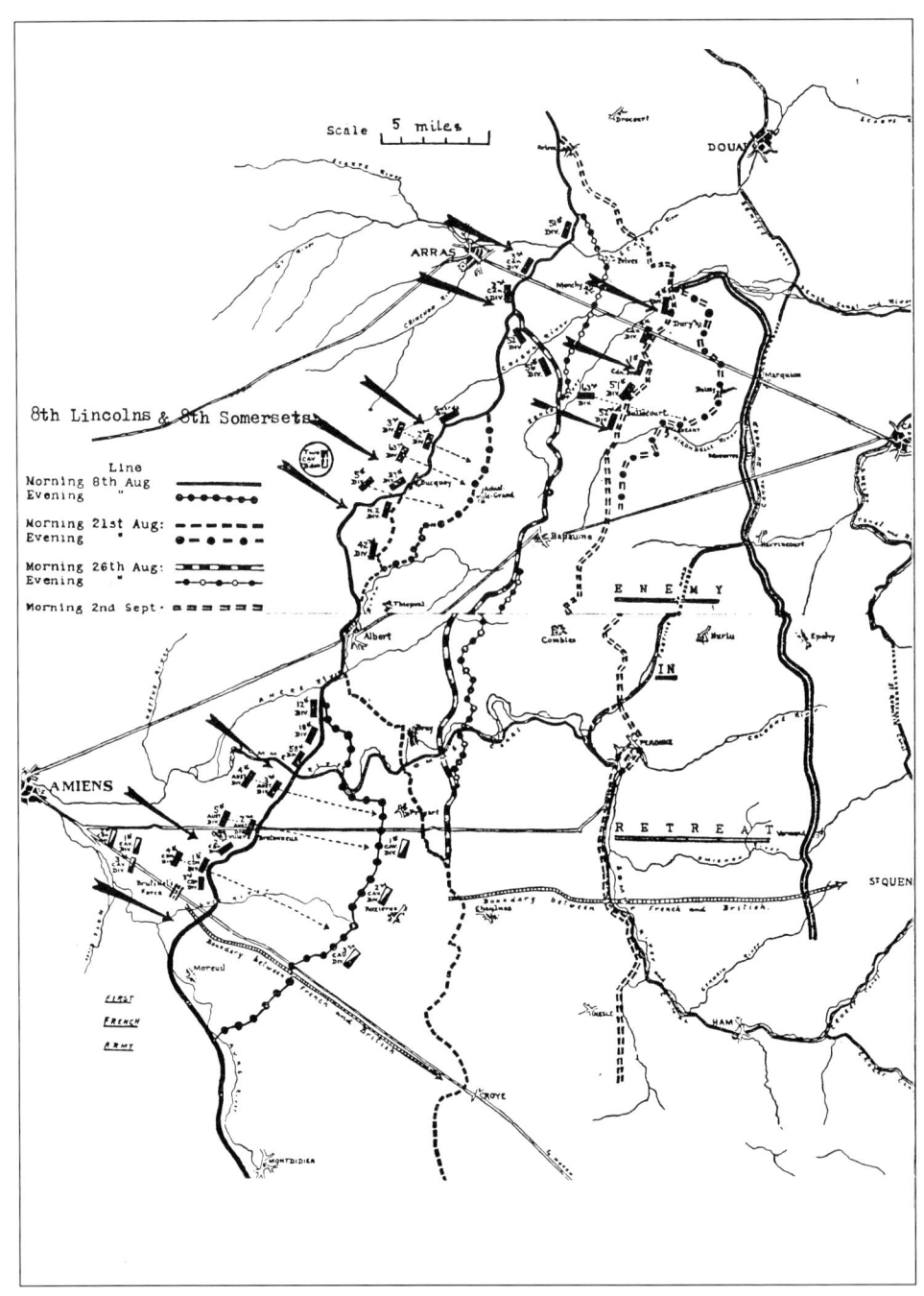

Opening of the Final British Offensive.
8th August - 9th September, 1918.

there that a new honour was conferred on Hardy. He was appointed a Chaplain to the King, an honour within the King's personal gift.

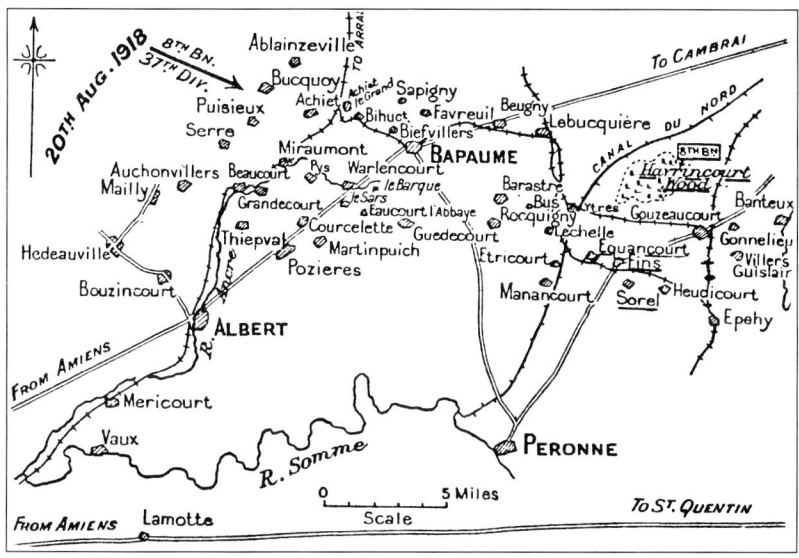

THE SECOND BATTLES OF THE SOMME, 1918.

The new C.O. of the 8th Somersets remembered the occasion:

'The news came that His Majesty the King desired the Padre to become one of his Chaplains in Ordinary. I remember so well his coming to me and shyly producing the letter from the Lord Chamberlain. The Regimental band was playing at the time; we were in rest billets for three days before again taking up the advance. There was a large throng of men gathered to hear the band. I collared the Padre, and took him along to where the band was playing, and, when the piece was finished, I announced to those present I had something to tell them. I told them I had found the Padre out, and then read out to them the letter from the Lord Chamberlain. Such a cheer went up as I shall always remember. The Padre was then called upon for a speech, and I shall never forget how he belittled his own doings — said that whilst he felt the honour of the favour which His Majesty had conferred on him, he felt that the honour was really conferred on the battalion, *not* on him. He was only afraid lest it might mean that he would be obliged to go home and leave his friends in the two battalions, if he accepted. He said that his greatest happiness in life was to be among his friends in the two battalions.'[1]

Hardy's comment that he might be obliged to go home hints at the pressure being put on him to do so. The King had been profoundly impressed by Hardy's record when he met him, and together with the Bishop of Carlisle, was the moving force behind an attempt to save him from further risk. The Bishop offered him the vacant living of Caldbeck (John Peel country in the Northern Lakeland Fells) at twice the income of

Officers of the 8th Battalion, the Lincolnshire Regiment, taken in January, 1919. Lieut-Colonel A. T. Hitch, D.S.O. is centre, front row.

Colonel Hitch was to write of Theodore Hardy: ' What his loss has meant to us is more than I can express, but his name will always be recalled with reverence, and to those of us who knew him really intimately, a great blank has appeared in our daily lives '.

Warrant Officers and Sergeants of the 8th Battalion, the Lincolnshire Regiment, at Frasnes-le-Gosselies in January, 1919 prior to demobilization.

Hutton Roof, but Hardy would not accept. The matter is recorded in the Carlisle Diocesan Gazette:

> 'The Bishop offered him the vacant rectory of Caldbeck, which, although most attractive to him by reason of his country tastes, love of natural beauty, fondness of country folk, delight in walking and climbing, he self-denyingly declined on the ground that as he had been absent from his little parish of Hutton Roof so long without any murmur from the parishioners, he felt it was his duty to return and serve them when the war was over.'[2]

His friend and colleague Geoffrey Vallings tried to get him to change his mind, but Hardy deflected him with a self-mocking comment:

> 'He hoped for his Majesty's sake that one of his duties as Honorary Chaplain would not be to preach for him.'[3]

The campaign continued, this time with Colonel Hitch, C.O. of the 8th Lincolns trying to influence him.

> 'I had a long talk with him as to the advisability of him accepting some post at the Base, a matter which I had talked over previously with the Divisional and Corps Chaplains, and which we were agreed was what ought to happen. He had done his bit we said, and now it was time for him to leave us for an easier life at the Base, where he could carry on his work backed by the enormous prestige his decorations had won him. Well, the Padre came back, and we started to talk about this work at the Base, but it was recognised from the start that my arguments would be useless, and I must admit that I was immensely pleased and proud to think that they were so. However, I stuck to it for some time, and finally I compromised and agreed to let the matter drop until the next time we came out of the line for a rest — but the occasion never came, for the next time we went into action was our advance up to the River Selle.'[4]

It should have come as no surprise that Hardy would not be moved. Two years of comradeship bound him to the men of the two battalions. Witness after witness speaks of his reluctance to leave the line. That was where he was happiest and that was where he was going to stay. Colonel Hitch remembers trying to find him:

> 'It was eleven o'clock at night and the Confirmation was to take place the next day at midday at the village about eight miles back; but the Padre could no-where be found. He was doing his round of posts, and it was only at four o'clock in the morning that we found him and packed him off to rear quarters. This was one of the many occasions when he went something like forty-eight hours without sleep. I have often wondered whether he managed to get a shave before meeting the Bishop, as he left us with four-days' growth.'[5]

Geoffrey Vallings remembers him collecting confirmation candidates:

'He literally pulled men out of the shell-hole line, going from one to the other, collecting them and walking down with them. Dead-beat, spent and weary, he arrived with that extraordinarily beautiful smile on his face, a veritable triumph of the spiritual over the physical.'[6]

* * * * *

The Bishop of Carlisle, no doubt prodded by the King, tried yet again. He wrote and asked Hardy to reconsider the offer of the living at Caldbeck. But Hardy would not shift. The most he would promise was to think the matter over and to consult Elizabeth. His reply to the Bishop ends:

> '. . . but perhaps I shall be called away soon, and there will be no need to make a decision.'[7]

And so it proved to be.

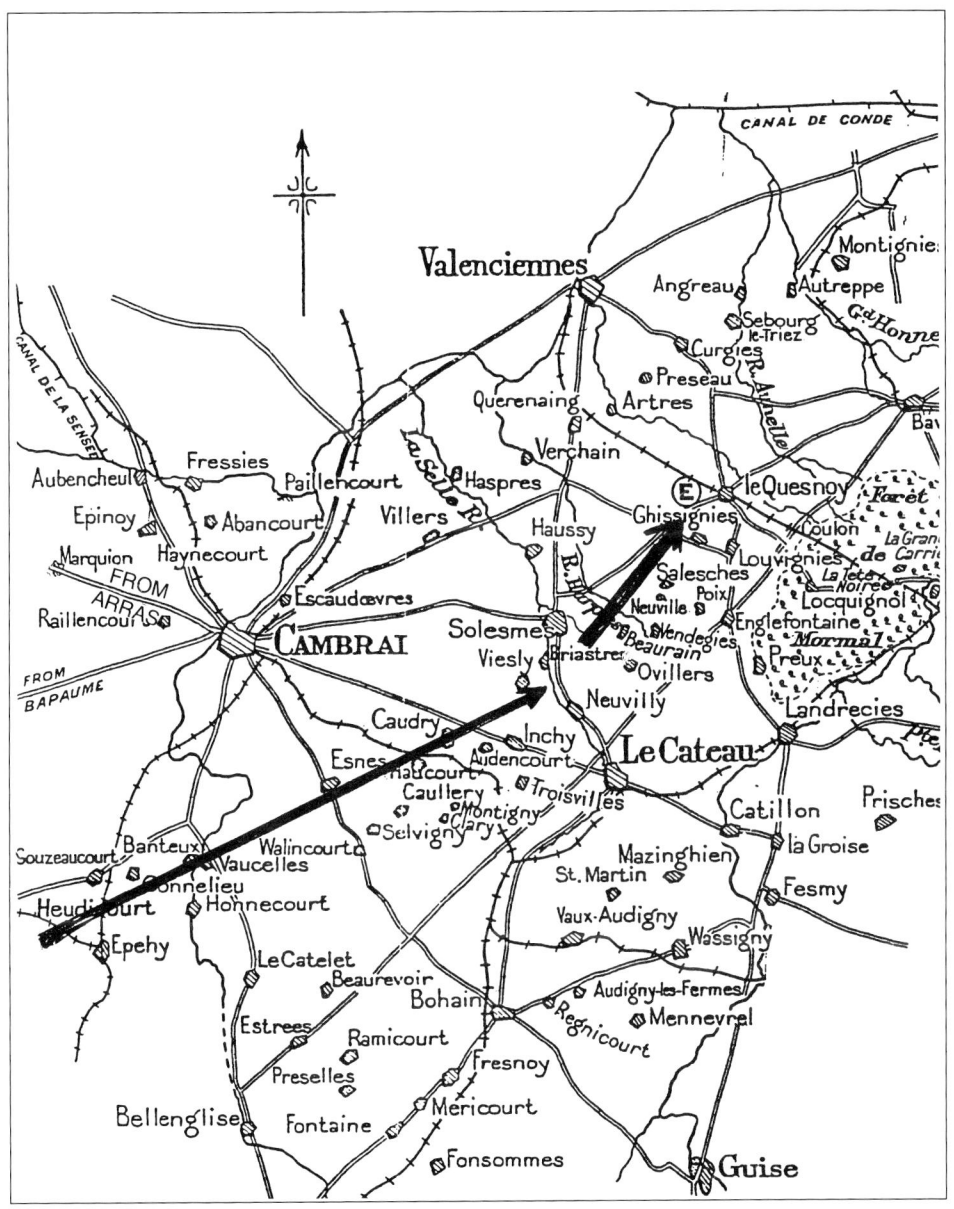

THE FINAL DAYS

Map taken from *The History of the Lincolnshire Regiment, 1914-1919.*

→ Line of advance by the 8th Lincolns and 8th Somersets in October, 1918.

Theodore Hardy was wounded crossing the River Selle at Briastres in the early hours of 11th October. The two Battalions saw only eight more days of action, and had reached point 'E' when the Armistice came into force on 11th November.

Private Jim Watson of the 8th Lincolns.

Private Watson volunteered soon after his 18th birthday in 1915. He served with the 8th Lincolns throughout Theodore Hardy's time with the battalion. He was in the team of Lewis Gunners and stretcher bearers crossing the River Selle when Hardy received his fatal wound. Jim Watson remembers Hardy saying, 'I've been hit. I'm sorry to be a nuisance.'

Private Watson still lives in Grantham, his home town.

On the 4th September, the Lincolns and the Somersets joined in the advance again. By this time the days of trench warfare were gone, and a war of movement had at last resumed. The Germans slowly retreated, but as the British followed them they were met with heavy machine-gun fire and artillery shelling. By the time they were relieved on 11th September, the two battalions had advanced another six miles to Havrincourt Wood but both had lost over 100 casualties. Yet they all felt that the end of the war was in sight, for the Germans were now in headlong retreat back towards their own frontier.

In the days that followed both battalions gave support to the advance troops as they went forward across the old Somme battlefields. The *History of the Somerset Light Infantry* gives a graphic description of what they saw:

> 'The utter desolation of the Somme country at this period was terrible to see. Gaping shell holes were everywhere, roads had been almost blotted out and had become mere tracks: villages that had once been the habitations of men no longer existed as such, tumbled masses of bricks and stones and rubbish marking the sites .... The holocausts of 1917 and 1918 ... had left this country bare and barren, a noisome place, the earth blood soaked and stinking with the rotting corpses which lay beneath its troubled surface. Everywhere traces of the beaten and defeated enemy were seen from the broken gun carriages, transport wagons, equipment and other abandoned war material, with the dead still crying silently for burial.'[8]

On the 8th October it was the turn of the Lincolns and Somersets to take on the brunt of the fighting yet again, for the Germans were still putting up fierce resistance in a fighting retreat. Their task was to attack to the south of Cambrai towards the River Selle; their stint was to last four days, and they faced a determined enemy:

> 'In spite of heavy machine-gun and artillery fire the advance went on ... machine-gunners raked the line of Somerset men. In the latter stages of the War the enemy's machine-gunners were the bravest troops in the German Army. With extraordinary tenacity they clung to every position ... They were brave fellows those German machine-gunners: they fought with their backs against the wall.'[9]

By nightfall of the 10th October, the two battalions which had fought alongside each other for over three years, were near the banks of the River Selle:

> 'When darkness had fallen all Companies sent out patrols to report any available crossings over the River Selle. They returned with the information that no crossings could be found, that the Selle was from twenty to thirty feet wide, and that there were no trees which could be felled for the construction of temporary bridges. But about 3.00 a.m. on 11th an officer of the 153rd Company, R.E., said that he would endeavour to erect some sort of bridge. B and C Companies of the 8th Somersets and one company of the Lincolns were then instructed ... to cross the river if ordered to do so. Soon the battalion had established its front on the eastern banks of the Selle, with the (Somersets) on the left and the Lincolns on the right.'[10]

The River Selle, October, 1918. On a bridge such as this just one mile away, Theodore Hardy received his fatal wound. The bridges were built by the Royal Engineers

In the darkness, a small figure looked across to the other side. He crossed the river to his friends. 'It's only me, boys' he said. After a while he told them he would have to go. Minutes later they heard the machine-gun open fire. They never saw him again, but he would stay with them always.

* * * * *

Theodore Hardy had been shot through the thigh, and at first it was hoped that his wound would not be too serious. His fellow stretcher bearers braved a hail of machine-gun bullets coming across the river to get him back to a dressing station. Private Maurice Calvert was there:

> 'He said to the stretcher bearers, in a voice husky with weakness and pain: "I'm sorry to give you all this trouble boys, when you are urgently needed elsewhere". His last thought as he was carried away was not for himself, you see.'[11]

In the First War, blood transfusion and intravenous fluid replacements were barely considered by the medical authorities. Many were to die from shock and loss of blood. Hardy was no exception, and no doubt the years of physical punishment and exhaustion were to play a part too.

He was evacuated by train, in itself an ordeal, over 100 miles to the No. 2 Red Cross Hospital at Rouen. Elizabeth was sent for. Douglas Carey, the Assistant Chaplain-General, saw him there:

> 'I saw him for a few moments. . . . Pneumonia had not yet set in, but he was very tired from his journey and not wholly conscious. He mistook me at first for his son, and called me by his pet name for his boy, who, he thought, might have turned up to see him.'[12]

He died a week after being wounded on 18th October. Three weeks later the war was over.

* * * * *

Douglas Carey, whom Theodore Hardy had badgered to be allowed to go up to the front, conducted the Funeral service. Six Chaplains acted as bearers. His old friend from the Kirkby Lonsdale Scout troop, Jonty Wilson, was there.

Back at the front, Colonel Sheringham had to break the news to the 8th Somersets:

> 'I shall never forget the expression of the men when the news came that the Padre was dead. There was an atmosphere of deep emotion. We all felt, I know, that we had all lost a very dear personal friend. Very few eyes were dry. This can easily be understood when one remembers that Padre Hardy was in very truth a brother to all

those young soldiers who now heard the news of his death. These lads were, like us all, very proud of him.'[13]

Colonel Hitch of the 8th Lincolns wrote to Mary Hardy:

'It was a tremendous shock when we heard that he had died. We had a short memorial service, and it was the most moving and sincere service I have ever attended . . . . The service was voluntary, and officers and men of nearly all the units with whom he had come into contact were there, though there was, of course, a majority of our men.

What his loss has meant to us is more than I can express, but his name will always be recalled with reverence, and to those of us who knew him really intimately, a great blank has appeared in our daily lives.'[14]

8th November, 1918.

Dear Sir,

The King and Queen have received with feelings of deep regret the news of the death of your Father, whose conspicuous and repeated acts of gallantry had already won him the V.C., the D.S.O., and the M.C.

The King much deplores the loss of so gallant an Officer, whose brilliant career has been a source of such pride and admiration among the whole of the Chaplains in the Army, and I am commanded to convey to you the expression of Their Majesties' true sympathy with you in your sorrow.

Yours very truly,

Keeper of the Privy Purse.

Captain W.H. Hardy, R.A.M.C.

THEODORE BAYLEY HARDY

Such a friend who is dead.
But relived. Stand. God, your train
...

G. R. V.

Poem written by the Rev. Geoffrey Vallings, D.S.O. when he heard of his close friend's death.[15]

[1] Sheringham, letter to Mary Hardy. opus cit.
[2] Carlisle Diocesan Gazette, November, 1918.
[3] Vallings, ibid.
[4] Hitch, ibid.
[5] Ibid.
[6] Vallings, ibid.
[7] Carlisle Diocesan Gazette, ibid.
[8] Wyrall, opus cit.
[9] Ibid.
[10] Ibid.
[11] Calvert, ibid.
[12] Carey, ibid.
[13] Sheringham, ibid.
[14] Hitch, ibid.
Theodore Bayley Hardy is buried in the Military Cemetery, St. Sever Extension, Rouen, France. Block S, Plot V, Row J, Grave 1.
[15] Original in possession of Miss Patricia Hardy. Geoffrey Vallings's poem was published in 'The Golden Horse Shoe', the Journal of the 37th Division, and had a few minor differences to the original:

Only a comrade is dead,
But relieved, thank God, from pain,
Ere he soared in flight
Far beyond our sight,
Where heroic spirits reign.

Only a Padre, and old
With an unassuming grace.
In his heart of gold
Was true courage bold,
And love-light shone in his face.

Only a pal of my own
On the road we twain have trod,
Till he passed alone
Through the great unknown
To shew me the way to God.

Only one man, just one more
In the roll of England's fame,
Yet his friends of yore
And the cross he wore
Are honoured by this man's name.

The Reverend G.R. Vallings, D.S.O., S.C.F.

Hutton Roof & Lupton.

December 1916

BURIAL.

Nov. 7—Betsy Bowness, aged 61 years.

I am taking advantage of the December Magazine to wish all in Hutton Roof and Lupton a happy or a hopeful Christmas—happy for some with its changeless message of peace to all of goodwill, while for those in anxiety or sorrow, the sure and certain hope, with its glorious healing power, which is ours through the great Christmas truth of "God made man for our sakes." It is my earnest prayer that the National Mission may have strengthened the hold of this truth upon our nation and that in that way lasting and growing good may come out of the sufferings of this present time.

T. B. HARDY, 53rd Brigade, B.E.F.

The Working Party at Lupton have made since their first meeting on Oct. 12th, 26 shirts, 24 pairs of socks, and 24 pairs of mittens: It has been decided to send each of the 28 men on the list a parcel containing socks, shirt, mittens, Oxo cubes, tea tablets, cake, cigarettes and sweets, or (in the case of those in hospital) its equivalent in money.

A local branch of the National War Savings Association has been formed in this parish. 90 members have already been enrolled, and a number of 15/6 certificates have been bought. It is earnestly hoped that the people of Lupton will largely avail themselves of this opportunity of saving and serving their country.

The Scripture Examination will take place on Wednesday, Dec. 6th, at 1-30 p.m.

Hutton Roof.

December 1917

We shall all heartily congratulate the Vicar of the Parish on the high military distinction he has gained as Chaplain of the Forces in France. The D.S.O. (Distinguished Service Order), ranks, I believe, in importance second only to the Victoria Cross. We have heard no details of the special gallantry which merited the award. Presumably the Decoration will be conferred upon Mr. Hardy when he is next on leave by the King personally at Buckingham Palace.

In response to a house-to-house collection for 'Xmas presents for the soldiers, a sum of £7 1s. has been raised. This, together with £1 18s. taken from Choir Funds, makes a total of £9.

We have pleasure in acknowledging and thanking Mr. Procter Gregg for a donation of £2 19s. towards our various Church Funds.

We have come to the end, and are entering upon a new year of grace on Advent Sunday, and amid the multitudinous claims which the modern world makes upon men's thoughts and occupations. The Festival of the Holy Birth of our Saviour, of which Advent is intended as a preparation, should shine out to the faithful with truer and deeper affection. We must offer to Him the undivided homage of our hearts on that blessed and Holy Day. To turn away from Him, whether nations or individuals, is to have no future. "The kingdom or nation that will not serve Thee," and may we reverently add the individual also, " shall perish." On the other hand, as one of our daily Collects teaches us, " to serve Him is to reign "

November 1918

Hutton Roof & Lupton.

We record the death of the Rev. T. B. Hardy, V.C., Vicar of the Parish. He was wounded in the leg on Friday, Oct. 11, and taken to a Red Cross Hospital in Rouen. Unfortunately pneumonia set in, after the wound seemed to be progressing favourably, and he died on Friday, Oct. 18, St. Luke's Day. Miss Hardy was able to be with him all the time, and only 1½ hours before his death he dictated a telegram asking for the Prayers of the Church for himself and all the wounded. The Chaplain of the hospital was in continuous attendance ministering to his spiritual needs. He was buried on Sunday, Oct. 20 On Wednesday, Oct. 23, a Solemn Eucharist was offered in Hutton Roof Church at 10-30 a.m., and in the afternoon a Service based on funeral office took place at which the parishioners generally were present. Simultaneously at Lupton a Service was taken by the Vicar of Whittington. Our hearts go out in loving sympathy to Dr and Miss Hardy. We feel persuaded they will be rejoicing in that Apostolic Comfort which S. Paul gives us, 1 Thess. IV. 13, a Scripture which was publicly read twice in Hutton Roof Church last Wednesday. May he, our dear brother, priest and Vicar of this Parish together with all the faithful departed, by God's mercy, rest in peace !

BURIAL.

Oct. 23.— George Charnley, aged 32.

He died in hospital at Glasgow and leaves a sorrowing widow to whom we offer our respectful sympathy.

We also offer our respectful sympathy to Mrs. Dodgson on her sad bereavement, the result of a fatal accident to her husband at the bottom of Church Lane. He was buried at Preston Patrick Church.

December 1918

Hutton Roof & Lupton.

The Curate in charge wishes to thank Miss Williams, Miss Bickersteth (Casterton) and Mr. Procter-Gregg and others for their charitable support in enabling us to have the assistance of a trained nurse and many other comforts during the late sickness, which is now happily abating.

It was our intention to present the late Vicar on his return from France with a gold watch and an illuminated address, subscribed for by practically every parishioner in the two parishes. This being now impossible, the watch (which was purchased at Bensons in London, of the value of £30), is to be given to the Vicar's son, Dr. W. Hardy and the illuminated address together with the small surplus cash is given to Miss Hardy. As many of us will be unable to see the address, we print it here on their behalf :—

TO THE

REVEREND T. B. HARDY, C.F., V.C., D.S.O., M.C.

Reverend Sir,

We, the undersigned, as representing your parishioners of Hutton Roof and Lupton beg your acceptance from us of a gold watch, together with this address, as a token of our admiration of your very distinguished services in France, as Chaplain of His Majesty's Forces. His Majesty the King, on the recommendation of the high Command in France, has duly recognised these services by bestowing upon you in succession the Distinguished Service Order, the Military Cross, and greatest of all the Victoria Cross. We cannot help feeling that a share of these honours is reflected upon ourselves. We hope you will live a long time to enjoy them and that Almighty God's Blessing and Protection will accompany you in your farther labours until this war is brought to a successful termination.

BAPTISM.

Nov. 17th.—Mabel daughter of John and Emma Amelia Mason.

BURIAL.

Oct. 25th.—John Staveley, aged 65 years.

Extracts from the Parish Magazine, Hutton Roof and Lupton.
1916 - 1918.